I0279757

J Brigel

A Grammar of the Tulu Language

J Brigel

A Grammar of the Tulu Language

ISBN/EAN: 9783743393516

Manufactured in Europe, USA, Canada, Australia, Japa

Cover: Foto ©Paul-Georg Meister /pixelio.de

Manufactured and distributed by brebook publishing software (www.brebook.com)

J Brigel

A Grammar of the Tulu Language

A GRAMMAR

OF THE

TULU LANGUAGE

BY

REV. J. BRIGEL
B. M. S.

MANGALORE
PUBLISHED BY C. STOLZ
BASEL MISSION BOOK & TRACT DEPOSITORY
1872

PRINTED BY STOLZ & REUTHER.

PREFATORY NOTE.

In offering to the public this first attempt at treating the Tuḷu Language grammatically, the Author and Publisher trust that it will be welcome to all who take an interest in the South Indian Languages, although they are well aware that a first work of this kind, written as this is, under a pressure of professional duties, cannot claim perfection.

Tuḷu is one of the Dravidian Languages, spoken only in the Collectorate of South Canara by about 500,000 people, and is nearly exactly confined between 12·30 and 13·30 degrees N. latitude, extending eastward to the foot of the Ghats. It cannot boast of any literature in the proper sense of the word, nor has it a character of its own. In writing, a modification of the Malayalam alphabet was used, till the Basel Mission Press employed Canarese characters in printing. This precedent has now been almost generally followed.

The first book ever printed in Tuḷu, is the Gospel of St. Matthew lithographed and published in 1842. Within 1847 the whole of the New Testament was finished, and a new typographical edition of it was issued in 1859. Besides this, the following was published at Mangalore: The Psalms, Liturgy, Hymn-Book, First and Second

Catechisms, Old and New Testament Bible Stories, Short Bible Stories, Prayer-Book, Flattich's Household-Rules, Congregation-Rules, Selection of Scripture Passages.

Special acknowledgment is due to A. Burnell Esq. M. C. S., who not only took much interest in the publication of this book, but facilitated it by a liberal donation towards the cost of printing.

Mangalore, 14*th September* 1872.

A

GRAMMAR OF THE TUḶU LANGUAGE

I. PART: PHONOLOGY.

1. Chapter: Of the Alphabet.

1. The Tuḷu language has no alphabet of its own. Those who formerly wrote in Tuḷu used to employ Malayālam characters; but more recently the Canarese alphabet has been adopted both in writing and printing; so the latter may now be considered as the modern Tuḷu alphabet.

2. In this alphabet there are 15 Vowels, two Medials and 34 Consonants.

A. Of Vowels.

3. Vowels are either short or long, or diphthongal or indefinite.

Short: ಅ a, ಇ i, ಉ u, ಋ ṛi, ಎ e, ಒ o.
Long: ಆ ā, ಈ ī, ಊ ū, ೠ ṛī, ಏ ē, ಓ ō.
Diphthongal: ಐ ei(ai), ಔ ou.
Indefinite: ‘ (as in ತ್), sounded nearly as the French e in je. Dr. Lepsius in his Standard Alphabet represents it by ụ.

B. Of Medials.

4. There are two Medials, viz: ಂ, which is sounded m, n, or ṅ according to position, and ಃ ah.

C. Of Consonants.

5. There are 25 classified and 9 unclassified Consonants, viz:—

Classified Consonants.

	Unaspirated.	Aspirated.	Unaspirated.	Aspirated.	Nasal.
Guttural Class	ಕ ka	ಖ kha	ಗ ga	ಘ gha	ಙ ṅa
Palatal	ಚ ča	ಛ čha	ಜ ja	ಝ jha	ಞ ńa
Cerebral	ಟ ṭa	ಠ ṭha	ಡ ḍa	ಢ ḍha	ಣ ṇa
Dental	ತ ta	ಥ tha	ದ da	ಧ dha	ನ na
Labial	ಪ pa	ಫ pha	ಬ ba	ಭ bha	ಮ ma

Unclassified Consonants.

ಯ ya, ರ ra, ಲ la, ವ va, ಶ ša, ಷ ša ಸ sa, ಹ ha, ಳ ḷa.

---

2. Chapter: Of Pronunciation.

TABULAR VIEW OF THE ALPHABET.

6. A. Vowels.

Initial forms.	Medial and final forms.	Corresponding English Characters.	Power of the Vowels.	Examples of Vowels and Consonants united
ಅ	‿	a	like a in about	ಕ್ and ಅ become ಕ ka
ಆ	ಾ	ā	„ a „ far	ಕ „ ಆ „ ಕಾ kā
ಇ	ಿ	i	„ i „ him	ಗ „ ಇ „ ಗಿ gi
ಈ	ೀ	ī	„ ee „ deep	ದ „ ಈ „ ದೀ dī
ಉ	ು	u	„ oo „ wool	ನ „ ಉ „ ನು nu
ಊ	ೂ	ū	„ oo „ cool	ಪ „ ಊ „ ಪೂ pū
ಋ	ೃ	ṛi		ಬ „ ಋ „ ಬೃ bṛi
ೠ	ೄ	ṛī		ಮ „ ೠ „ ಮೄ mṛī
ಎ	ೆ	e	„ e „ met	ಯ „ ಎ „ ಯೆ ye
ಏ	ೇ	ē	„ a „ mate	ರ „ ಏ „ ರೇ rē
ಐ	ೈ	ei	„ y „ my	ಲ „ ಐ „ ಲೈ lei
ಒ	ೊ	o	„ o „ not	ಶ „ ಒ „ ಶೊ šo
ಓ	ೋ	ō	„ o „ note	ಸ „ ಓ „ ಸೋ sō
ಔ	ೌ	ou	„ ow „ owl	ಹ „ ಔ „ ಹೌ hou

The vowels are pronounced according to the directions given in the preceding tabular view of the alphabet, except ಎ e, ಏ ē, ಒ o, ಓ ō, which when initials are pronounced ye, yē, wo, wō; as, ಎಣ್ಮ yeṇma, ಏತ್ yētṳ, ಒಂಜಿ wonji, ಓಡ wōḍa. In ಋ ṛi, ೠ ṛī, the i and ī have the short and long sound of the French eu in beurre.

7. B. Consonants.

Consonants with the inherent vowel ಅ a.	Corresponding English Characters.	Sound of the Consonants with the inherent vowel ಅ a.	Form and position when combined with other consonants	EXAMPLES.	
ಕ ಕ	ka	like ka in kalendar	್ಕ	ಮುಸ್ಕು	musku
ಖ ಖ	kha	*	್ಖ	ಪಸ್ಖ	paskha
ಗ ಗ	ga	„ ga „ gander	್ಗ	ಸದ್ಗುಣ	sadguṇa
ಘ ಘ	gha	*	್ಘ	ಮೇಲ್ಘಟ್ಟ	mēlghaṭṭa
ಙ ಙ	ṅa	*	್ಙ	ಙಙೆ	ṅaṅe
ಚ ಚ	ča	„ cha „ chapter	್ಚ	ನಿಶ್ಚಯ	niščaya
ಛ ಛ	čha	*	್ಛ	ಇಚ್ಛೆ	iččhe
ಜ ಜ	ja	„ ja „ jam	್ಜ	ಸಜ್ಜಿ	sajji
ಝ ಝ	jha	*	್ಝ		
ಞ ಞ	ńa	„ nya „ bunyan	್ಞ	ಜ್ಞಾನ	jńána
ಟ ಟ	ṭa	„ rta „ martaban	್ಟ	ಕಷ್ಟ	kašṭa
ಠ ಠ	ṭha	*	್ಠ	ಷಷ್ಠಿ	šašṭhi
ಡ ಡ	ḍa	„ rda „ cardamom	್ಡ	ಬಡ್ಡಿ	baḍḍi
ಢ ಢ	ḍha	*	್ಢ	ದೃಢ	dṛiḍha
ಣ ಣ	ṇa	*	್ಣ	ಪಟ್ಣ	patṇa
ತ ತ	ta	„ ta „ tank	್ತ	ದುಸ್ತು	dustu
ಥ ಥ	tha	*	್ಥ	ಸ್ಥಳ	sthaḷa
ದ ದ	da	„ tha „ that	್ದ	ಮಳ್ತೊಣ್ದು	maḷtoṇdu
ಧ ಧ	dha	*	್ಧ	ಸಿದ್ಧ	siddha
ನ ನ	na	„ na „ natural	್ನ	ಪ್ರಯತ್ನ	prayatna
ಪ ಪ	pa	„ pa „ parrot	್ಪ	ಇನ್ಪಿ	inpi
ಫ ಫ	pha	*	್ಫ	ಸ್ಫಟಿಕ	sphaṭika
ಬ ಬ	ba	„ ba „ barrow	್ಬ	ಬೊಬ್ಬೆ	bobbe
ಭ ಭ	bha	*	್ಭ	ಸದ್ಭಕ್ತಿ	sadbhakti
ಮ ಮ	ma	„ ma „ matter	್ಮ	ಆತ್ಮ	ātma
ಯ ಯ	ya	„ ya „ yam	್ಯ	ಅನ್ಯಾಯ	anyāya
ರ ರ	ra	„ ra „ rag	್ರ	ಪ್ರಾಣ	prāṇa
ಲ ಲ	la	„ la „ lack	್ಲ	ಮಾತೆರ್ಲಾ	māterlā
ವ ವ	va	„ va „ van	್ವ	ಸತ್ವ	satva
ಶ ಶ	śa	„ sha „ sham	್ಶ		
ಷ ಷ	ša	„ sha „ marshal	್ಷ	ವರ್ಷ	varša
ಸ ಸ	sa	„ sa „ sat	್ಸ	ಮತ್ಸರ	matsara
ಹ ಹ	ha	„ ha „ ham	್ಹ	ಮಧ್ಯಾನ್ಹ	madhyānha
ಳ ಳ	ḷa		್ಳ	ಕಟ್ಳೆ	kaṭḷe

* The preceding sound aspirated.

ಅ a	ಆ ā	ಇ i	ಈ ī	ಉ u	ಊ ū	ಋ ṛi	ೠ ṛī
ಕ ka	ಕಾ kā	ಕಿ ki	ಕೀ kī	ಕು ku	ಕೂ kū	ಕೃ kṛi	ಕೄ kṛī
ಖ kha	ಖಾ khā	ಖಿ khi	ಖೀ khī	ಖು khu	ಖೂ khū	ಖೃ khṛi	ಖೄ khṛī
ಗ ga	ಗಾ gā	ಗಿ gi	ಗೀ gī	ಗು gu	ಗೂ gū	ಗೃ gṛi	ಗೄ gṛī
ಘ gha	ಘಾ ghā	ಘಿ ghi	ಘೀ ghī	ಘು ghu	ಘೂ ghū	ಘೃ ghṛi	ಘೄ ghṛī
ಙ ṅa	ಙಾ ṅā	ಙಿ ṅi	ಙೀ ṅī	ಙು ṅu	ಙೂ ṅū	ಙೃ ṅṛi	ಙೄ ṅṛī
ಚ ča	ಚಾ čā	ಚಿ či	ಚೀ čī	ಚು ču	ಚೂ čū	ಚೃ čṛi	ಚೄ čṛī
ಛ čha	ಛಾ čhā	ಛಿ čhi	ಛೀ čhī	ಛು čhu	ಛೂ čhū	ಛೃ čhṛi	ಛೄ čhṛī
ಜ ja	ಜಾ jā	ಜಿ ji	ಜೀ jī	ಜು ju	ಜೂ jū	ಜೃ jṛi	ಜೄ jṛī
ಝ jha	ಝಾ jhā	ಝಿ jhi	ಝೀ jhī	ಝು jhu	ಝೂ jhū	ಝೃ jhṛi	ಝೄ jhṛī
ಞ ńa	ಞಾ ńā	ಞಿ ńi	ಞೀ ńī	ಞು ńu	ಞೂ ńū	ಞೃ ńṛi	ಞೄ ńṛī
ಟ ṭa	ಟಾ ṭā	ಟಿ ṭi	ಟೀ ṭī	ಟು ṭu	ಟೂ ṭū	ಟೃ ṭṛi	ಟೄ ṭṛī
ಠ ṭha	ಠಾ ṭhā	ಠಿ ṭhi	ಠೀ ṭhī	ಠು ṭhu	ಠೂ ṭhū	ಠೃ ṭhṛi	ಠೄ ṭhṛī
ಡ ḍa	ಡಾ ḍā	ಡಿ ḍi	ಡೀ ḍī	ಡು ḍu	ಡೂ ḍū	ಡೃ ḍṛi	ಡೄ ḍṛī
ಢ ḍha	ಢಾ ḍhā	ಢಿ ḍhi	ಢೀ ḍhī	ಢು ḍhu	ಢೂ ḍhū	ಢೃ ḍhṛi	ಢೄ ḍhṛī
ಣ ṇa	ಣಾ ṇā	ಣಿ ṇi	ಣೀ ṇī	ಣು ṇu	ಣೂ ṇū	ಣೃ ṇṛi	ಣೄ ṇṛī
ತ ta	ತಾ tā	ತಿ ti	ತೀ tī	ತು tu	ತೂ tū	ತೃ tṛi	ತೄ tṛī
ಥ tha	ಥಾ thā	ಥಿ thi	ಥೀ thī	ಥು thu	ಥೂ thū	ಥೃ thṛi	ಥೄ thṛī
ದ da	ದಾ dā	ದಿ di	ದೀ dī	ದು du	ದೂ dū	ದೃ dṛi	ದೄ dṛī
ಧ dha	ಧಾ dhā	ಧಿ dhi	ಧೀ dhī	ಧು dhu	ಧೂ dhū	ಧೃ dhṛi	ಧೄ dhṛī
ನ na	ನಾ nā	ನಿ ni	ನೀ nī	ನು nu	ನೂ nū	ನೃ nṛi	ನೄ nṛī
ಪ pa	ಪಾ pā	ಪಿ pi	ಪೀ pī	ಪು pu	ಪೂ pū	ಪೃ pṛi	ಪೄ pṛī
ಫ pha	ಫಾ phā	ಫಿ phi	ಫೀ phī	ಫು phu	ಫೂ phū	ಫೃ phṛi	ಫೄ phṛī
ಬ ba	ಬಾ bā	ಬಿ bi	ಬೀ bī	ಬು bu	ಬೂ bū	ಬೃ bṛi	ಬೄ bṛī
ಭ bha	ಭಾ bhā	ಭಿ bhi	ಭೀ bhī	ಭು bhu	ಭೂ bhū	ಭೃ bhṛi	ಭೄ bhṛī
ಮ ma	ಮಾ mā	ಮಿ mi	ಮೀ mī	ಮು mu	ಮೂ mū	ಮೃ mṛi	ಮೄ mṛī
ಯ ya	ಯಾ yā	ಯಿ yi	ಯೀ yī	ಯು yu	ಯೂ yū	ಯೃ yṛi	ಯೄ yṛī
ರ ra	ರಾ rā	ರಿ ri	ರೀ rī	ರು ru	ರೂ rū	ರೃ rṛi	ರೄ rṛī
ಲ la	ಲಾ lā	ಲಿ li	ಲೀ lī	ಲು lu	ಲೂ lū	ಲೃ lṛi	ಲೄ lṛī
ವ va	ವಾ vā	ವಿ vi	ವೀ vī	ವು vu	ವೂ vū	ವೃ vṛi	ವೄ vṛī
ಶ śa	ಶಾ śā	ಶಿ śi	ಶೀ śī	ಶು śu	ಶೂ śū	ಶೃ śṛi	ಶೄ śṛī
ಷ ša	ಷಾ šā	ಷಿ ši	ಷೀ šī	ಷು šu	ಷೂ šū	ಷೃ šṛi	ಷೄ šṛī
ಸ sa	ಸಾ sā	ಸಿ si	ಸೀ sī	ಸು su	ಸೂ sū	ಸೃ sṛi	ಸೄ sṛī
ಹ ha	ಹಾ hā	ಹಿ hi	ಹೀ hī	ಹು hu	ಹೂ hū	ಹೃ hṛi	ಹೄ hṛī
ಳ ḷa	ಳಾ ḷā	ಳಿ ḷi	ಳೀ ḷī	ಳು ḷu	ಳೂ ḷū	ಳೃ ḷṛi	ಳೄ ḷṛī

ಎ e	ಏ ē	ಐ ei	ಒ o	ಓ ō	ಔ ou	ಂ am	ಃ ah
ಕೆ ke	ಕೇ kē	ಕೈ kei	ಕೊ ko	ಕೋ kō	ಕೌ kou	ಕಂ kam	ಕಃ kah
ಖೆ khe	ಖೇ khē	ಖೈ khei	ಖೊ kho	ಖೋ khō	ಖೌ khou	ಖಂ kham	ಖಃ khah
ಗೆ ge	ಗೇ gē	ಗೈ gei	ಗೊ go	ಗೋ gō	ಗೌ gou	ಗಂ gam	ಗಃ gah
ಘೆ ghe	ಘೇ ghē	ಘೈ ghei	ಘೊ gho	ಘೋ ghō	ಘೌ ghou	ಘಂ gham	ಘಃ ghah
ಙೆ ṅe	ಙೇ ṅē	ಙೈ ṅei	ಙೊ ṅo	ಙೋ ṅō	ಙೌ ṅou	ಙಂ ṅam	ಙಃ ṅah
ಚೆ če	ಚೇ čē	ಚೈ čei	ಚೊ čo	ಚೋ čō	ಚೌ čou	ಚಂ čam	ಚಃ čah
ಛೆ čhe	ಛೇ čhē	ಛೈ čhei	ಛೊ čho	ಛೋ čhō	ಛೌ čhou	ಛಂ čham	ಛಃ čhah
ಜೆ je	ಜೇ jē	ಜೈ jei	ಜೊ jo	ಜೋ jō	ಜೌ jou	ಜಂ jam	ಜಃ jah
ಝೆ jhe	ಝೇ jhē	ಝೈ jhei	ಝೊ jho	ಝೋ jhō	ಝೌ jhou	ಝಂ jham	ಝಃ jhah
ಞೆ ńe	ಞೇ ńē	ಞೈ ńei	ಞೊ ńo	ಞೋ ńō	ಞೌ ńou	ಞಂ ńam	ಞಃ ńah
ಟೆ ṭe	ಟೇ ṭē	ಟೈ ṭei	ಟೊ ṭo	ಟೋ ṭō	ಟೌ ṭou	ಟಂ ṭam	ಟಃ ṭah
ಠೆ ṭhe	ಠೇ ṭhē	ಠೈ ṭhei	ಠೊ ṭho	ಠೋ ṭhō	ಠೌ ṭhou	ಠಂ ṭham	ಠಃ ṭhah
ಡೆ ḍe	ಡೇ ḍē	ಡೈ ḍei	ಡೊ ḍo	ಡೋ ḍō	ಡೌ ḍou	ಡಂ ḍam	ಡಃ ḍah
ಢೆ ḍhe	ಢೇ ḍhē	ಢೈ ḍhei	ಢೊ ḍho	ಢೋ ḍhō	ಢೌ ḍhou	ಢಂ ḍham	ಢಃ ḍhah
ಣೆ ṇe	ಣೇ ṇē	ಣೈ ṇei	ಣೊ ṇo	ಣೋ ṇō	ಣೌ ṇou	ಣಂ ṇam	ಣಃ ṇah
ತೆ te	ತೇ tē	ತೈ tei	ತೊ to	ತೋ tō	ತೌ tou	ತಂ tam	ತಃ tah
ಥೆ the	ಥೇ thē	ಥೈ thei	ಥೊ tho	ಥೋ thō	ಥೌ ṭhou	ಥಂ tham	ಥಃ thah
ದೆ de	ದೇ dē	ದೈ dei	ದೊ do	ದೋ dō	ದೌ dou	ದಂ dam	ದಃ dah
ಧೆ dhe	ಧೇ dhē	ಧೈ dhei	ಧೊ dho	ಧೋ dhō	ಧೌ dhou	ಧಂ dham	ಧಃ dhah
ನೆ ne	ನೇ nē	ನೈ nei	ನೊ no	ನೋ nō	ನೌ nou	ನಂ nam	ನಃ nah
ಪೆ pe	ಪೇ pē	ಪೈ pei	ಪೊ po	ಪೋ pō	ಪೌ pou	ಪಂ pam	ಪಃ pah
ಫೆ phe	ಫೇ phē	ಫೈ phei	ಫೊ pho	ಫೋ phō	ಫೌ phou	ಫಂ pham	ಫಃ phah
ಬೆ be	ಬೇ bē	ಬೈ bei	ಬೊ bo	ಬೋ bō	ಬೌ bou	ಬಂ bam	ಬಃ bah
ಭೆ bhe	ಭೇ bhē	ಭೈ bhei	ಭೊ bho	ಭೋ bhō	ಭೌ bhou	ಭಂ bham	ಭಃ bhah
ಮೆ me	ಮೇ mē	ಮೈ mei	ಮೊ mo	ಮೋ mō	ಮೌ mou	ಮಂ mam	ಮಃ mah
ಯೆ ye	ಯೇ yē	ಯೈ yei	ಯೊ yo	ಯೋ yō	ಯೌ you	ಯಂ yam	ಯಃ yah
ರೆ re	ರೇ rē	ರೈ rei	ರೊ ro	ರೋ rō	ರೌ rou	ರಂ ram	ರಃ rah
ಲೆ le	ಲೇ lē	ಲೈ lei	ಲೊ lo	ಲೋ lō	ಲೌ lou	ಲಂ lam	ಲಃ lah
ವೆ ve	ವೇ vē	ವೈ vei	ವೊ vo	ವೋ vō	ವೌ vou	ವಂ vam	ವಃ vah
ಶೆ še	ಶೇ šē	ಶೈ šei	ಶೊ šo	ಶೋ šō	ಶೌ šou	ಶಂ šam	ಶಃ šah
ಷೆ še	ಷೇ šē	ಷೈ šei	ಷೊ šo	ಷೋ šō	ಷೌ šou	ಷಂ šam	ಷಃ šah
ಸೆ se	ಸೇ sē	ಸೈ sei	ಸೊ so	ಸೋ sō	ಸೌ sou	ಸಂ sam	ಸಃ sah
ಹೆ he	ಹೇ hē	ಹೈ hei	ಹೊ ho	ಹೋ hō	ಹೌ hou	ಹಂ ham	ಹಃ hah
ಳೆ ḷe	ಳೇ ḷē	ಳೈ ḷei	ಳೊ ḷo	ಳೋ ḷō	ಳೌ ḷou	ಳಂ ḷam	ಳಃ ḷah

The following fourteen Consonants are pronounced like the English letters by which they are represented: ಕ ka, ಗ ga, ಚ ča, ಜ ja, ಪ pa, ಬ ba, ಮ ma, ಯ ya, ರ ra, ಲ la, ವ va, nearly ಶ śa, ಸ sa, ಹ ha.

8. The remaining Consonants do not correspond to the letters of the English alphabet. The following are dental letters; they must be pronounced with the tip of the tongue between the front teeth: ತ ta, ಥ tha, ದ da, ಧ dha, ನ na.

9. The following are cerebral letters:—

ಟ ṭa, ಠ ṭha, ಡ ḍa, ಢ ḍha, ಣ ṇa; ಷ ša, ಳ ḷa.

(Tables showing the alphabet with the combinations of the Vowels and Consonants).

c. Syllables.

10. The short vowel is inherent in the initial or complete form of every consonant; so that every letter is capable of being a complete syllable. Thus: ಕುರುಬ ku-ru-be, shepherd; ಅಮಸರ a-ma-sa-ra, haste; ಕಾಡ್ kā-ḍu, forest.

11. When a syllable is formed of two or more consonants and one vowel, the vowel is always joined to the first or uppermost consonant, but sounded after the last or lowest one; thus: ಕ್ಲಿ kli, ತ್ಯು tyu, ಸ್ತ್ರೀ strī.

ಕ್ಕ—ಅಕ್ಕ; ಡ್ಗ—ಖಡ್ಗ; ಶ್ಚ—ನಿಶ್ಚಯ; ಚ್ಛೆ—ಇಚ್ಛೆ; ಜ್ಜೆ—ಅಜ್ಜೆ; ಜ್ಞಾ—ಜ್ಞಾನ; ಟ್ಟ—ಕಟ್ಟಳೆ; ಷ್ಟ—ಕಷ್ಟ; ಟ್ಣ—ಪಟ್ಣ; ಷ್ಣ—ಉಷ್ಣ; ಡ್ಡಿ—ಅಡ್ಡಿ; ಸ್ತ—ಪುಸ್ತಕ; ಸ್ಥಿ—ಸ್ಥಿತಿ; ಬ್ದ—ಶಬ್ದ; ದ್ಧ—ಅಶುದ್ಧ; ತ್ನ—ಪ್ರಯತ್ನ; ತ್ಪ—ಉತ್ಪನ್ನ; ತ್ಮ—ಆತ್ಮ; ಜ್ಯ—ರಾಜ್ಯ; ತ್ರ—ಗಾಂತ್ರ; ಗ್ಲೆ—ಬಂಗ್ಲೆ; ತ್ವ—ಯಾಜಕತ್ವ; ಕ್ಸ—ಲುಕ್ಸಾನ್; ಸ್ತ್ರ—ಶಾಸ್ತ್ರ.

12. The half letter ರ್ r is pronounced before the letter or syllable which in writing precedes it; thus: ವರ್ಗ varga, class; ಕರ್ತವೆ kartave, Lord; ಹೊರ್ತಂದೆ hortande, except.

d. Double Consonants.

13. Most of the consonants are capable of reduplication, as with unchanged form of under-written consonants:

1. ಖ್ಖ; ಜ್ಜ; ಞ್ಞ; ಣ್ಣ; ಬ್ಬ.

With partially changed form of under-written consonants:

2. ಕ್ಕ; ಗ್ಗ; ಘ್ಘ; ಚ್ಚ; ಛ್ಛ; ಟ್ಟ; ಠ್ಠ; ಡ್ಡ; ಢ್ಢ; ಥ್ಥ; ಧ್ಧ; ಪ್ಪ; ಫ್ಫ; ಭ್ಭ; ವ್ವ; ಶ್ಶ; ಷ್ಷ; ಸ್ಸ; ಹ್ಹ; ಳ್ಳ.

With entirely changed form of under-written consonants:

3. ತ್ತ; ನ್ನ; ಮ್ಮ; ಯ್ಯ; ರ್ರ; ಲ್ಲ.

---

3. Chapter: Of Euphony.

14. Euphony occasions the elision, insertion, and permutation of letters.

a. Elision.

15. When a word ending in ಅ a, ಇ i, ಉ u, or ‘ ŭ is followed by an affix commencing with a vowel, euphony requires elision as follows:

ಪ್ರೀತಿದ+ಆಕುಳು=ಪ್ರೀತಿದಾಕುಳು; ಬೇಲೆದ+ಆಕುಳು=ಬೇಲೆದಾಕುಳು; ತೂದು+ಇತ್ತೆ=ತೂದಿತ್ತೆ; ಗೊಂತು+ಇಜ್ಜಿ=ಗೊಂತಿಜ್ಜಿ; ಬರೆದ್+ಆಂಡ್ ಬರೆದಾಂಡ್ etc.

b. Insertion.

16. Sometimes ನ್ n is inserted; as, ಧೊರೆ+ನ್+ಆಕುಳು=ಧೊರೆನಾಕುಳು; ಅಮ್ಮ+ನ್+ಆಕುಳು=ಅಮ್ಮನಾಕುಳು.

c. Permutation.

17. In compound words sometimes the consonant is changed; as, ಕಾರ್ಗತ್ತಲೆ instead of ಕಾರ್ಕತ್ತಲೆ; ವಾಗ್ದಂಡ for ವಾಕ್ದಂಡ; ಅಂಗೈ for ಅಂಗಕೈ; ಮುಂಗೈ for ಮುನ್ಕೈ.

Remark: In the declensions of nouns and pronouns hard and soft consonants are, for the sake of euphony, frequently exchanged; as, ಕುರಿತ for ಕುರಿದ; ನೆಲತ for ನೆಲದ; ಕುರಿಕ್ for ಕುರಿಗ್; ನೆಲೊಟು for ನೆಲೊಡು.

II. PART: ETYMOLOGY.

1. Chapter: Of the Formation of Words.

DISTINCTION OF WORDS ACCORDING TO THEIR ORIGIN.

18. The Tuḷuvas have adopted many words from the languages, they have come in contact with; here we find in their vocabulary *a.*, pure Tuḷu, *b.*, pure Sanscrit, *c.*, corrupted Sanscrit, *d.*, Canarese, *e.*, Hindustāny and *f.*, foreign words.

Examples of pure Tuḷu words: ಇಲ್ಲ್ illụ, house; ಬಂಜಿ banji, belly; ಪಾತೆರ pātera, word; ಯೆಡ್ಡೆ yeḍḍe, good; ಪಡಿಕೆ paḍike, bad; etc.

Examples of pure Sanscrit: ಪ್ರೀತಿ prīti, love; ನೀತಿ nīti, justice; ಗುರು guru, master.

Examples of corrupted Sanscrit: ಪ್ರಶ್ನೆ praśne, question (ಪ್ರಶ್ನಾ praśnā); ಸೊನ್ನೆ sonne, ೦; ಬೋಧನೆ (ಬೋಧನಾ) bōdhane, advice.

Examples of (pure) Canarese: ಶೆರೆಮನೆ śeremane, confinement; ಹೊಟ್ಟೆಕಿಚ್ಚಿ hoṭṭekichchi, envy; ತಿಳುವಳಿಕೆ tiḷuvaḷike, knowledge.

Examples of Hindustāny: ಕಾಲಿ (ಖಾಲಿ) kāli (khāli) empty; ಖಾಸಿ (ಖಾಸ) khāsi (khāsa), own; ಕುಷಿ (ಖುಶಿ, ಖುಷಿ) kuśi (khuśi, khuśi), (will) glad.

Examples of foreign words: ಸಲಾಂ (ಸಲಾಮು) salām (salāmu); ಕೋರ್ಟ್ cōrṭụ, court; ಕಲ್ಲಕಟರ್ kallakaṭarụ, collector.

DISTINCTION OF WORDS ACCORDING TO THEIR FORM.

19. There are Primitive, Derivative and Compound Words.

a. Primitive Words.

1. Verbs: ನಂಬು nambu, believe; ಕಟ್ಟು kaṭṭu, build.
2. Nouns: ಮರ mara, tree; ಕಲ್ಲ್ kallụ, stone; ನೆಲ nela, ground, etc.
3. Pronouns: ಯಾನ್ yānụ, I; ಆ ā, that; ಇಂಚಿ inči, hither.
4. Numerals: ಒಂಜಿ wonji, one; ಪತ್ತ್ pattụ, ten; ಪಾಕ pāka, some; ನೂದು nūdu, hundred, etc.

b. Derivative Words.

1. Verbal derivatives: as, ನಂಬಿಗೆ nambige, trust (ನಂಬು nambu, believe); ತಾಳ್ಮೆ tāḷme, patience (from ತಾಳು); ಕಟ್ಟ katta and ಕಟ್ಟೆ katte, bundle (from ಕಟ್ಟು kattu).

2. Other derivatives:

a) Ending in ತ್ವ tva, ತನ tana, ಗೆ ge: as, ಬುದ್ಧಿಹೀನತ್ವ buddhihīnatva, stupidity; ಯೆಡ್ಡೆತನ yeḍḍetana, goodness; ಮಲ್ಲಾದಿಗೆ mallādige, greatness.

b) Ending in ಗಾರೆ gāre, ವಂತೆ vante, ಇ i, ಇಷ್ಟೆ ište, ಸ್ಥೆ sthe, ಕೆ ke: as, ಮೋಸಗಾರೆ mōsagāre, deceiver; ಬುದ್ಧಿವಂತೆ buddhivante, wise man; ವ್ಯಭಿಚಾರಿ vyabhiċāri, an adulterer; ಪಾಪಿಷ್ಟೆ pāpište, a sinner; ವ್ಯಾಪಾರಸ್ಥೆ vyāpārasthe, a merchant, a seller; ಬೋಧಕೆ bōdhake, a teacher.

c) Ending in ಳ್ ḷu̥, ದಿ di: as, ಮಗಳ್ magaḷu̥, a daughter; ಮೋಸಗಾರೆದಿ mōsagāredi, a deceitful woman.

C. Compound Words.

20. Compound words may be formed by the union of two nouns or by affixing pronouns to the genitive case of nouns and to participles, as will be seen from the following examples.

a) Union of two nouns: ಹಿರೆಕೂಟ hirekūṭa, presbytery; ನೀರ್ ಕುತ್ತ nīru̥kutta, dropsy; ಪಾಪಪರಿಹಾರ pāpaparihāra, forgiveness of sin.

21. *b*) Affixing pronouns to the genitive case of nouns: ಪ್ರೀತಿದಾಯೆ prītidāye (ಪ್ರೀತಿದ+ಆಯೆ prītida+āye), lover; ಪ್ರೀತಿದಾಳ್ prītidāḷu̥ (ಪ್ರೀತಿದ+ಆಳ್ prītida+āḷu̥); ಪ್ರೀತಿದಾಕುಳು prītidākuḷu (ಪ್ರೀತಿದ+ಆಕುಳು prītida+ākuḷu), lovers; ಪಟ್ಣದಾಯೆ paṭṇadāye (ಪಟ್ಣದ paṭṇada + ಆಯೆ āye,—ಆಳ್ āḷu̥,—ಅವು avu,—ಆಕುಳು ākuḷu,—ಐಕುಳು eikuḷu), citizen.

c) Affixing pronouns to participles which, for the sake of euphony, requires the insertion of the letter ನ್ nu̥: ಮಳ್ಪುನಾಯೆ maḷpunāye (ಮಳ್ಪು maḷpu+ನ್ nu̥+ಆಯೆ āye,—ಆಳ್ āḷu̥,—ಅವು avu) maker or one that makes; ಮಳ್ಪುನಾಕುಳು maḷpunākuḷu (ಮಳ್ಪು maḷpu+ನ್ nu̥+ಆಕುಳು ākuḷu,—ಐಕುಳು eikuḷu) makers or things that make; ಬತ್ತಿನಾಯೆ battināye (ಬತ್ತಿ batti+ನ್ nu̥+ಆಯೆ āye,—ಆಳ್ āḷu̥,—ಅವು avu), one that came; ಬತ್ತಿನಾಕುಳು battināku!u (ಬತ್ತಿ batti+ನ್ nụ+ಆಕುಳು āku!u,-ಐಕುಳು eiku!u), persons or things that came.

2. Chapter: Of Parts of Speech.

22. There are five principal parts of speech viz: Nouns, Pronouns, Numerals, Verbs and Particles.

FIRST SECTION: NOUNS.

23. Nouns are of three kinds, viz: Substantive, Adjective, and Adverbial.

1. OF SUBSTANTIVES.

a. Gender of Substantives.

24. Substantives are of three Genders: Masculine, Feminine, and Neuter.

25. The names of men and gods are Masculine, those of women and goddesses Feminine, animals and inanimate objects are generally Neuter. The word ಆಣ್ aṇụ, male, is often prefixed to show the male sex; as, ಆಣ್ಬಾಲೆ āṇụbāle, a male infant; ಆಣ್ಪಿಲಿ āṇụpili, a tiger.

26. The word ಪೊಣ್ಣು poṇṇu, female is often prefixed to show the female sex; as, ಪೊಣ್ಣುಬಾಲೆ poṇṇubāle, a female child; ಪೊಣ್ಣುಪಿಲಿ poṇṇupili, a tigress.

27. There are some exceptions to the above rule; thus: ಬಾಲೆ bāle, a child, is generally and ಜನ jana, a person or people, frequently Neuter; as, ಬಾಲೆ ಪುಟ್ಟ್ಂಡ್ bāle puṭṭụnḍụ, a child is born; ಜನ ಬತ್ತ್ಂಡ್ jana battụndụ, the people have come.

b. Number of Substantives.

28. Substantives have two numbers: Singular and Plural.

29. The Plural is formed by adding 'ರ್ rụ' or 'ಳು ḷụ' or 'ಕುಳು ku!u' to the singular; as, ಕರ್ತವೆ kartave, lord, ಕರ್ತವೆರ್ kartaverụ, lords; ಮೇಜಿ mēji, table, ಮೇಜಿಳು mējiḷu, tables; ಕುರಿ kuri, sheep, ಕುರಿಕುಳು kuriku!u, sheep.

30. Plural Substantives of relationship terminate in ಆಡ್ಳು ādḷu; as, ಅಮ್ಮಾಡ್ಳು ammādḷu, fathers; ಸಹೋದ್ರಿಯಾಡ್ಳು sahōdriyādḷu, sisters.

31. When the cardinal numbers are used in reference to persons, the word ಜನ jana may be added to ಒಂಜಿ wonji, one, and either ಜನ or ಮಂದೆ mande to all the other numbers; thus: ಒಂಜಿ ಜನ wonji jana, one person; ರಡ್ಡ್ ಜನ raḍḍụ jana or ರಡ್ಡ್ ಮಂದೆ raḍḍụ mande, two persons.

c. Declension of Substantives.

32. Substantives have 8 Cases viz: Nominative, Genitive, Dative, Accusative, Locative, Ablative or Instrumental, Communicative and Vocative. Of these the Nominative singular is the same as the crude form of the word; the formation of the Nominative plural has been explained in the preceding paragraph, the remaining cases are formed by adding affixes to the Nominative.

Cases.	Affixes.	
	Singular.	*Plural.*
1. *Nominative*	ಅ a, ವು u, ಎ e etc.	ರ್ rụ, ಳು ḷu, ಕುಳು kuḷu
2. *Genitive*	ಅ a, ತ ta, ದ da	ರೆ re, ಳೆ ḷe
3. *Dative*	ಗ್ g, ಕ್ kụ, ಗು gu, ಕು ku	ರೆಗ್ regụ
4. *Accusative*	ನ್ nụ, ನು nu	ರೆ re, ಳೆನ್ ḷenụ
5. *Locative*	ಡ್ ḍụ, ಟ್ ṭụ, ಡು ḍu, ಟು ṭu	ಳೆಡ್ ḷeḍụ
6. *Ablative or Instru.*	ಡ್ದ್ ḍụdụ, ಡ್ದು ḍụdu	ಳೆಡ್ದ್ ḷeḍụdụ
7. *Communicative*	ಡ ḍa, ಟ ṭa	ಳೆಡ ḷeḍa
8. *Vocative*	ಆ ā, ಓ ō	ರೇ rē, ಳೇ ḷē

33. There are 5 declensions or modes of forming the cases of substantives by adding the above-mentioned affixes, varying principally according to the termination of words in their crude form. They are therefore conveniently termed *a.*, declension in ಅ a; *b.*, declension in ಇ i; *c.*, declension in ಉ u; *d.*, declension in ಎ e, and *e.*, declension in ʻ ụ.

34. I. Declension:

1st EXAMPLE.

1. Personal noun—Crude form:

Singular.

1. *Nom.*	ಅಮ್ಮ amma, a mistress.
2. *Genit.*	ಅಮ್ಮ amma, of a mistress.
3. *Dat.*	ಅಮ್ಮಗ್ ammagu̥, to a mistress.
4. *Accus.*	ಅಮ್ಮನ್ ammanu̥, a mistress.
5. *Locat.*	ಅಮ್ಮಡ್ ammaḍu̥, in a mistress.
6. *Ablat.*	ಅಮ್ಮಡ್ದ್ ammaḍu̥du̥, from, by or through a mistress.
7. *Comm.*	ಅಮ್ಮಡ ammaḍa, to a mistress.
8. *Vocat.*	ಅಮ್ಮಾ ammā, O mistress!

35. 2nd EXAMPLE.

2. Impersonal nouns—*a.*, Crude form: ಜೀವ jīva, life

Singular.

1. *Nom.*	ಜೀವ jīva, life.
2. *Gen.*	ಜೀವದ jīvada, of life.
3. *Dat.*	ಜೀವೊಗು jīvogu, to life.
4. *Accus.*	ಜೀವೊನು jīvonu, life.
5. *Locat.*	ಜೀವೊಡು jīvoḍu, in life.
6. *Ablat.*	ಜೀವೊಡ್ದು jīvoḍu̥du, from, by or through life.
7. *Comm.*	ಜೀವಡ jīvaḍa, to life.
8. *Vocat.*	ಜೀವಾ jīvā, O life!

Substantive ending in ಅ a.

ಅಮ್ಮ amma, a mistress.

Plural.

ಅಮ್ಮನಾಕುಳು ammanākuḷu, mistresses.

ಅಮ್ಮನಾಕುಳೆ ammanākuḷe, of mistresses.

ಅಮ್ಮನಾಕುಳೆಗ್ ammanākuḷegu̦, to mistresses.

ಅಮ್ಮನಾಕುಳೆನ್ ammanākuḷenu̦, mistresses.

ಅಮ್ಮನಾಕುಳೆಡ್ ammanākuḷeḍu̦, in mistresses.

ಅಮ್ಮನಾಕುಳೆಡ್ದ್ ammanākuḷeḍu̦du̦, from, by or through mistresses.

ಅಮ್ಮನಾಕುಳೆಡ ammanākuḷeḍa, to mistresses.

ಅಮ್ಮನಾಕುಳೇ ammanākuḷē, O mistresses!

(with the soft consonants).

Plural.

ಜೀವೊಳು jīvoḷu, lives.

ಜೀವೊಳೆ jīvoḷe, of lives.

ಜೀವೊಳೆಗ್ jīvoḷegu̦, to lives.

ಜೀವೊಳೆನ್ jīvoḷenu̦, lives.

ಜೀವೊಳೆಡ್ jīvoḷeḍu̦, in lives.

ಜೀವೊಳೆಡ್ದ್ jīvoḷeḍu̦du̦, from, by or through lives.

ಜೀವೊಳೆಡ jīvoḷeḍa, to lives.

ಜೀವೊಳೇ jīvoḷē, O lives!

36. 3RD EXAMPLE.

b., Crude form: ಮರ **mara**, a tree

Singular.

1. *Nom.*	ಮರ **mara**, a tree.
2. *Gen.*	ಮರತ **marata**, of a tree.
3. *Dat.*	ಮರೊಕು **maroku**, to a tree.
4. *Accus.*	ಮರೊನು **maronu**, a tree.
5. *Locat.*	ಮರೊಟು **maroṭu**, in a tree.
6. *Ablat.*	ಮರೊಡ್ದು **maroḍḍu**, from, by or through a tree.
7. *Comm.*	ಮರಟ **maraṭa**, to a tree.
8. *Vocat.*	ಮರಾ **marā**, O tree!

37. II. Declension:

1ST EXAMPLE.

1. Personal nouns—Crude form:

Singular.

1. *Nom.*	ಪ್ರವಾದಿ **pravādi**, a prophet.
2. *Gen*	ಪ್ರವಾದಿ **pravādi**, of a prophet.
3. *Dat.*	ಪ್ರವಾದಿಗ್ **pravādigụ**, to a prophet.
4. *Accus.*	ಪ್ರವಾದಿನ್ **pravādinụ**, a prophet.
5. *Locat.*	ಪ್ರವಾದಿಡ್ **pravādiḍụ**, in a prophet.
6. *Ablat.*	ಪ್ರವಾದಿಡ್ದ್ **pravādiḍḍụ**, from, by or through a prophet.
7. *Comm.*	ಪ್ರವಾದಿಡ **pravādiḍa**, to a prophet.
8. *Vocat.*	ಪ್ರವಾದಿಯೇ **pravādiyē**, O prophet!

(with the hard consonants).

Plural.

ಮರೊಕುಳು marokuḷu, trees.

ಮರೊಕುಳೆ marokuḷe, of trees.

ಮರೊಕುಳೆಗ್ marokuḷegu̥, to trees.

ಮರೊಕುಳೆನ್ marokuḷenu̥, trees.

ಮರೊಕುಳೆಡ್ marokuḷeḍu̥, in trees.

ಮರೊಕುಳೆಡ್ದ್ marokuḷeḍu̥du̥, from, by or through trees.

ಮರೊಕುಳೆಡ marokuḷeḍa, to trees.

ಮರೊಕುಳೇ marokuḷē, O trees!

Substantive ending in ಇ e.

ಪ್ರವಾದಿ pravādi, a prophet.

Plural.

ಪ್ರವಾದಿಳು pravādiḷu, prophets.

ಪ್ರವಾದಿಳೆ pravādiḷe, of prophets.

ಪ್ರವಾದಿಳೆಗ್ pravādiḷegu̥, to prophets.

ಪ್ರವಾದಿಳೆನ್ pravādiḷenu̥, prophets.

ಪ್ರವಾದಿಳೆಡ್ pravādiḷeḍu̥, in prophets.

ಪ್ರವಾದಿಳೆಡ್ದ್ pravādiḷeḍu̥du̥, from, by or through prophets.

ಪ್ರವಾದಿಳೆಡ pravādiḷeḍa, to prophets.

ಪ್ರವಾದಿಳೇ pravādiḷē, O prophets!

Crude form: ನರಮಾನಿ **naramāni**, a man.

Singular.

1.	*Nom.*	ನರಮಾನಿ **naramāni**, a man.
2.	*Gen.*	ನರಮಾನ್ಯ **naramānya**, of a man.
3.	*Dat.*	ನರಮಾನ್ಯಗ್ **naramānyagu̥**, to a man.
4.	*Accus.*	ನರಮಾನ್ಯನ್ **naramānyanu̥**, a man.
5.	*Locat.*	ನರಮಾನ್ಯಡ್ **naramānyaḍu̥**, in a man.
6.	*Ablat.*	ನರಮಾನ್ಯಡ್ದ್ **naramānyaḍu̥du̥**, from, by or through a man.
7.	*Comm.*	ನರಮಾನ್ಯಡ **naramānyaḍa**, to a man.
8.	*Vocat.*	ನರಮಾನ್ಯಾ **naramānyā** O man!

38. 2ND EXAMPLE.

2. Impersonal nouns—*a.*, Crude form:

Singular.

1.	*Nom.*	ಮೇಜಿ **mēji**, a table.
2.	*Gen.*	ಮೇಜಿದ **mējida**, of a table.
3.	*Dat.*	ಮೇಜಿಗ್ **mējigu̥**, to a table.
4.	*Accus.*	ಮೇಜಿನ್ **mējinu̥**, a table.
5.	*Locat.*	ಮೇಜಿಡ್ **mējiḍa**, in a table.
6.	*Ablat.*	ಮೇಜಿಡ್ದ್ **mējiḍu̥du̥**, from, through or by a table.
7.	*Comm.*	ಮೇಜಿಡ **mējiḍa**, to a table.
8.	*Vocat.*	ಮೇಜಿಯೇ **mējiyē**, O table!

Plural

ನರಮಾನ್ಯೆರ್ **naramānyerụ**, men.

ನರಮಾನ್ಯೆರೆ **naramānyere**, of men.

ನರಮಾನ್ಯೆರೆಗ್ **naramānyeregụ**, to men.

ನರಮಾನ್ಯೆರೆನ್ **naramānyerenụ**, men.

ನರಮಾನ್ಯೆರೆಡ್ **naramānyereḍụ**, in men.

ನರಮಾನ್ಯೆರೆಡ್ದ್ **naramānyereḍụdụ**, from, by or through men.

ನರಮಾನ್ಯೆರೆಡ **naramānyereḍa**, to men.

ನರಮಾನ್ಯೆರೇ **naramānyerē**, O men!

ಮೇಜಿ **mēji**, a table (with soft consonants).

Plural.

ಮೇಜಿಳು **mējiḷu**, tables.

ಮೇಜಿಳೆ **mējiḷe**, of tables.

ಮೇಜಿಳೆಗ್ **mējiḷegụ**, to tables.

ಮೇಜಿಳೆನ್ **mējiḷenụ**, tables.

ಮೇಜಿಳೆಡ್ **mējiḷeḍụ**, in tables.

ಮೇಜಿಳೆಡ್ದ್ **mējiḷeḍụdụ**, from, through or by tables.

ಮೇಜಿಳೆಡ **mējiḷeḍa**, to tables.

ಮೇಜಿಳೇ **mējiḷē**, O tables!

39. 3RD EXAMPLE.

b., Crude form: ಕುರಿ kuri, a sheep

Singular.

1. *Nom.*	ಕುರಿ kuri, a sheep.
2. *Gen.*	ಕುರಿತ kurita, of a sheep.
3. *Dat.*	ಕುರಿಕ್ kuriku̥, to a sheep.
4. *Accus.*	ಕುರಿನ್ kurinu̥, a sheep.
5. *Locat.*	ಕುರಿಟ್ kuriṭu̥, in a sheep.
6. *Ablat.*	ಕುರಿಡ್ದ್ kuriḍu̥du̥, from, by or through a sheep.
7. *Comm.*	ಕುರಿಟ kuriṭa, to a sheep.
8. *Vocat.*	ಕುರಿಯೋ kuriyō, O sheep!

40. III. Declension:

1ST EXAMPLE.

1. Personal noun—Crude form:

Singular.

1. *Nom.*	ಗುರು guru, a priest.
2. *Gen.*	ಗುರು guru, of a priest.
3. *Dat.*	ಗುರುಕು guruku, to a priest.
4. *Accus.*	ಗುರುನು gurunu, a priest.
5. *Locat.*	ಗುರುಟು guruṭu, in a priest.
6. *Ablat.*	ಗುರುಡ್ದು guruḍu̥du, from, by or through a priest.
7. *Comm.*	ಗುರುಟ guruṭa, to a priest.
8. *Vocat.*	ಗುರೋ gurō, ಗುರುವೇ guruvē, O priest!

(with hard consonants).

Plural.

ಕುರಿಕುಳು kuriku̥lu, sheep.

ಕುರಿಕುಳೆ kurikuḷe, of sheep.

ಕುರಿಕುಳೆಗ್ kurikuḷegṳ, to sheep.

ಕುರಿಕುಳೆನ್ kurikuḷenṳ, sheep.

ಕುರಿಕುಳೆಡ್ kurikuḷeḍṳ, in sheep.

ಕುರಿಕುಳೆಡ್ದ್ kurikuḷeḍṳdṳ, from, by or through sheep.

ಕುರಿಕುಳೆಡ kurikuḷeḍa, to sheep.

ಕುರಿಕುಳೇ kurikuḷē, O sheep!

Substantive ending in ಉ u.

ಗುರು guru, a priest.

Plural.

ಗುರುಕುಳು gurukuḷu, priests.

ಗುರುಕುಳೆ gurukuḷe, of priests.

ಗುರುಕುಳೆಗ್ gurukuḷegṳ, to priests.

ಗುರುಕುಳೆನ್ gurukuḷenṳ, priests.

ಗುರುಕುಳೆಡ್ gurukuḷeḍṳ, in priests.

ಗುರುಕುಳೆಡ್ದ್ gurukuḷeḍṳdṳ, from, by or through priests.

ಗುರುಕುಳೆಡ gurukuḷeḍa, to priests.

ಗುರುಕುಳೇ gurukuḷē, O priests!

41. 2ND EXAMPLE.

2. Impersonal nouns—*a.*, Crude form:

Singular.

1. *Nom.*	ಬೊಳ್ಪು boḷpu, light.
2. *Gen.*	ಬೊಳ್ಪದ boḷpuda, of light.
3. *Dat.*	ಬೊಳ್ಪುಗು boḷpugu, to light.
4. *Accus.*	ಬೊಳ್ಪುನು boḷpunu, light.
5. *Locat.*	ಬೊಳ್ಪುಡು boḷpuḍu, in light.
6. *Ablat.*	ಬೊಳ್ಪುಡ್ಡು boḷpuḍḍu, from, by or through light.
7. *Comm.*	ಬೊಳ್ಪಡ boḷpuḍa, to light.
8. *Vocat.*	ಬೊಳ್ಪೋ boḷpō, O light!

42. 3RD EXAMPLE.

b., Crude form: ಪೂ pū, a flower

Singular.

1. *Nom.*	ಪೂ pū, a flower.
2. *Gen.*	ಪೂತ pūta, of a flower.
3. *Dat.*	ಪೂಕು pūku, to a flower.
4. *Accus.*	ಪೂನು pūnu, a flower.
5. *Locat.*	ಪೂಟು pūṭu, in a flower.
6. *Ablat.*	ಪೂಡ್ಡು pūḍḍu, from, by or through a flower.
7. *Comm.*	ಪೂಟ pūṭa, to a flower.
8. *Vocat.*	ಪೂ pū, O flower!

ಬೊಳ್ಪು bo̤lpu, light (with soft consonants).

Plural.

ಬೊಳ್ಪುಳು bo̤lpṳlu, lights.

ಬೊಳ್ಪುಳೆ bo̤lpṳle, of lights.

ಬೊಳ್ಪುಳೆಗ್ bo̤lpṳlegu̥, to lights.

ಬೊಳ್ಪುಳೆನ್ bo̤lpṳlenu̥, lights.

ಬೊಳ್ಪುಳೆಡ್ bo̤lpṳleḍu̥, in lights.

ಬೊಳ್ಪುಳೆಡ್ದ್ bo̤lpṳleḍu̥du̥, from, by or through lights.

ಬೊಳ್ಪುಳೆಡ bo̤lpṳleḍa, to lights.

ಬೊಳ್ಪುಳೇ bo̤lpṳlē, O lights!

(with hard consonants).

Plural.

ಪೂಕುಳು pūkṳlu, flowers.

ಪೂಕುಳೆ pūkṳle, of flowers.

ಪೂಕುಳೆಗ್ pūkṳlegu̥, to flowers.

ಪೂಕುಳೆನ್ pūkṳlenu̥, flowers.

ಪೂಕುಳೆಡ್ pūkṳleḍu̥, in flowers.

ಪೂಕುಳೆಡ್ದ್ pūkṳleḍu̥du̥, from, by or through flowers.

ಪೂಕುಳೆಡ pūkṳleḍa, to flowers.

ಪೂಕುಳೇ pūkṳlē, O flowers!

43. IV. Declension:

1st EXAMPLE.

1. Personal noun—Crude form:

Singular.

1. *Nom.*	ಕರ್ತವೆ kartave, a lord.
2. *Gen.*	ಕರ್ತವ kartava, of a lord.
3. *Dat.*	ಕರ್ತವಗ್ kartavagu̥, to a lord.
4. *Accus.*	ಕರ್ತವನ್ kartavanu̥, a lord.
5. *Locat.*	ಕರ್ತವಡ್ kartavaḍu̥, in a lord.
6. *Ablat.*	ಕರ್ತವಡ್ದ್ kartavaḍu̥du̥, from, by or through a lord.
7. *Comm.*	ಕರ್ತವಡ kartavaḍa, to a lord.
8. *Vocat.*	ಕರ್ತವಾ kartavā, O lord!

44. 2nd EXAMPLE.

2. Impersonal nouns—*a.*, Crude form:

Singular.

1. *Nom.*	ಬೇಲೆ bēle, work.
2. *Gen.*	ಬೇಲೆದ bēleda, of work.
3. *Dat.*	ಬೇಲೆಗ್ bēlegu̥, to work.
4. *Accus.*	ಬೇಲೆನ್ bēlenu̥, work.
5. *Locat.*	ಬೇಲೆಡ್ bēleḍu̥, in work.
6. *Ablat.*	ಬೇಲೆಡ್ದ್ bēleḍu̥du̥, from, by or through work.
7. *Comm.*	ಬೇಲೆಡ bēleḍa, to work.
8. *Vocat.*	ಬೇಲೇ bēlē, O work!

Substantive ending in ಎ.

ಕರ್ತವೆ **kartave,** a lord.

Plural.

ಕರ್ತವೆರ್ **kartaverụ, lords.**

ಕರ್ತವೆರೆ **kartavere, of lords.**

ಕರ್ತವೆರೆಗ್ **kartaveregụ, to lords.**

ಕರ್ತವೆರೆನ್ **kartaverenụ, lords.**

ಕರ್ತವೆರೆಡ್ **kartavereḍụ, in lords.**

ಕರ್ತವೆರೆಡ್ದ್ **kartavereḍụdụ, from, by or through lords.**

ಕರ್ತವೆರೆಡ **kartavereḍa, to lords.**

ಕರ್ತವೆರೇ **kartaverē, O lords!**

ಬೇಲೆ **bēle,** work.

Plural.

ಬೇಲೆಳು **bēleḷu, works.**

ಬೇಲೆಳೆ **bēleḷe, of works.**

ಬೇಲೆಳೆಗ್ **bēleḷegụ, to works.**

ಬೇಲೆಳೆನ್ **bēleḷenụ, works.**

ಬೇಲೆಳೆಡ್ **bēleḷeḍụ, in works.**

ಬೇಲೆಳೆಡ್ದ್ **bēleḷeḍụdụ, from, by or through works.**

ಬೇಲೆಳೆಡ **bēleḷeḍa, to works.**

ಬೇಲೆಳೇ **bēleḷē, O works!**

3RD EXAMPLE.

b., Crude form: ಕುದಿಕೆ **kudike**, a fox.

Singular.

1. *Nom.*	ಕುದಿಕೆ **kudike**, a fox.
2. *Gen.*	ಕುದಿಕ **kudika**, of a fox.
3. *Dat.*	ಕುದಿಕಗ್ **kudikagụ**, to a fox.
4. *Accus.*	ಕುದಿಕನ್ **kudikanụ**, a fox.
5. *Locat.*	ಕುದಿಕಡ್ **kudikaḍụ**, in a fox.
6. *Ablat.*	ಕುದಿಕಡ್ದ್ **kudikaḍụdụ**, from, by or through a fox.
7. *Comm.*	ಕುದಿಕಡ **kudikaḍa**, to a fox.
8. *Vocat.*	ಕುದಿಕಾ **kudikā**, O fox!

45. 4TH EXAMPLE.

c., Crude form: ತರೆ **tare**, a head

Singular.

1. *Nom.*	ತರೆ **tare**, a head.
2. *Gen.*	ತರೆತ **tareta**, of a head.
3. *Dat.*	ತರೆಕ್ **tarekụ**, to a head.
4. *Accus.*	ತರೆನ್ **tarenụ**, a head.
5. *Locat.*	ತರೆಟ್ **tareṭụ**, in a head.
6. *Ablat.*	ತರೆಡ್ದ್ **tareḍụdụ**, from, by or through a head.
7. *Comm.*	ತರೆಟ **tareṭa**, to a head.
8. *Vocat.*	ತರೇ **tarē**, O head!

(with a peculiar plural form "ೞು rḷu").

Plural.

ಕುದಿಕೆೞು **kudikerḷu**, foxes.

ಕುದಿಕೆೞೆ **kudikerḷe**, of foxes.

ಕುದಿಕೆೞೆಗ್ **kudikerḷegụ**, to foxes.

ಕುದಿಕೆೞೆನ್ **kudikerḷenụ**, foxes.

ಕುದಿಕೆೞೆಡ್ **kudikerḷeḍụ**, in foxes.

ಕುದಿಕೆೞೆಡ್ದ್ **kudikerḷeḍụdụ**, from, by or through foxes.

ಕುದಿಕೆೞೆಡ **kudikerḷeḍa**, to foxes.

ಕುದಿಕೆೞೇ **kudikerḷē**, O foxes!

(with the hard consonants).

Plural.

ತರೆಳು **tareḷu**, heads.

ತರೆಳೆ **tareḷe**, of heads.

ತರೆಳೆಗ್ **tareḷegụ**, to heads.

ತರೆಳೆನ್ **tareḷenụ**, heads.

ತರೆಳೆಡ್ **tareḷeḍụ**, in heads.

ತರೆಳೆಡ್ದ್ **tareḷeḍụdụ**, from, by or through heads.

ತರೆಳೆಡ **tareḷeḍa**, to heads.

ತರೆಳೇ **tareḷē**, O heads!

Most of the Masculine Proper Names are declined according to the 4th Declension.

46. V. Declension:

1st EXAMPLE.

1. Personal nouns—*a*., Crude form:

Singular.

1. *Nom.*	ಆಣ್ āṇụ, a boy.
2. *Gen.*	ಆಣಾ āṇa, of a boy.
3. *Dat.*	ಆಣಾಗ್ āṇagụ, to a boy.
4. *Accus.*	ಆಣಾನ್ āṇanụ, a boy.
5. *Locat.*	ಆಣಾಡ್ āṇaḍụ, in a boy.
6. *Ablat.*	ಆಣಾಡ್ದ್ āṇaḍụdụ, from, by or through a boy.
7. *Comm.*	ಆಣಾಡ āṇaḍa, to a boy
8. *Vocat.*	ಆಣೇ āṇē, O boy!

47. 2nd EXAMPLE.

b., Crude form:

Singular.

1. *Nom.*	ದೇವೆರ್ dēverụ, God.
2. *Gen.*	ದೇವೆರೆ dēvere, of God.
3. *Dat.*	ದೇವೆರೆಗ್ dēveregụ, to God.
4. *Accus.*	ದೇವೆರೆನ್ dēverenụ, God.
5. *Locat.*	ದೇವೆರೆಡ್ dēvereḍụ, in God.
6. *Ablat.*	ದೇವೆರೆಡ್ದ್ dēvereḍụdụ, from, by or through God.
7. *Comm.*	ದೇವೆರೆಡ dēvereḍa, to God.
8. *Vocat.*	ದೇವೆರೇ dēverē, O God!

Substantive ending in ⁶ ṳ.

ಆಣ್ āṇṳ, a boy.

Plural.

ಆಣುಳು āṇuḷu, boys.
ಆಣುಳೆ āṇuḷe, of boys.
ಆಣುಳೆಗ್ āṇuḷegṳ, to boys.
ಆಣುಳೆನ್ āṇuḷenṳ, boys.
ಆಣುಳೆಡ್ āṇuḷeḍṳ, in boys.
ಆಣುಳೆಡ್ದ್ āṇuḷeḍṳdṳ, from, by or through boys.
ಆಣುಳೆಡ āṇuḷeḍa, to boys.
ಆಣುಳೇ āṇuḷē, O boys!

ದೇವೆರ್ dēverṳ, God.

Plural.

ದೇವೆರುಳು dēveruḷu, gods.
ದೇವೆರುಳೆ dēveruḷe, of gods.
ದೇವೆರುಳೆಗ್ dēveruḷegṳ, to gods.
ದೇವೆರುಳೆನ್ dēveruḷenṳ, gods.
ದೇವೆರುಳೆಡ್ dēveruḷeḍṳ, in gods.
ದೇವೆರುಳೆಡ್ದ್ dēveruḷeḍṳdṳ, from, by or through gods.
ದೇವೆರುಳೆಡ dēveruḷeḍa, to gods.
ದೇವೆರುಳೇ dēveruḷē, O gods!

Remark: Though ದೇವೆರ್ dēveru̥ is a plural form, a second

48. 3rd EXAMPLE.

2. Impersonal noun—Crude form:

Singular.

1. *Nom.*	ಮದ್ Ϝ mardu̥, a medicine.
2. *Gen.*	ಮದ್ Ϝ ಬ mardu̥da, of a medicine.
3. *Dat.*	ಮದ್ Ϝ ಗ್ mardu̥gu̥, to a medicine.
4. *Accus.*	ಮದ್ Ϝ ನ್ mardu̥nu̥, a medicine.
5. *Locat.*	ಮದ್ Ϝ ಡ್ mardu̥du̥, in a medicine.
6. *Ablat.*	ಮದ್ Ϝ ಡ್ದ್ mardu̥du̥du̥, from, by or through a medicine.
7. *Comm.*	ಮದ್ Ϝ ಡ mardu̥da, to a medicine.
8. *Vocat.*	ಮದೋϜ mardō, O medicine!

NOUNS OF

49. Nouns of Relationship require the addition of nouns of relationship ending in ಅ a are declined like like nouns of 2nd Declension.

a., Crude form:

Singular.

1. *Nom.*	ಅಮ್ಮೆ amme, a father.
2. *Gen.*	ಅಮ್ಮ amma, of a father.
3. *Dat.*	ಅಮ್ಮಗ್ ammagu̥, to a father.
	&c. &c.

plural is formed by affixing ಳು ḷu.

ಮದ್ರ್ mardụ, a medicine.

Plural.

ಮದ್ರ್ಳು marduḷu, medicines.

ಮದ್ರ್ಳೆ marduḷe, of medicines.

ಮದ್ರ್ಳೆಗ್ marduḷegụ, to medicines.

ಮದ್ರ್ಳೆನ್ marduḷenụ, medicines.

ಮದ್ರ್ಳೆಡ್ marduḷeḍụ, in medicines.

ಮದ್ರ್ಳೆಡ್ದ್ marduḷeḍụdụ, from, by or through medicines.

ಮದ್ರ್ಳೆಡ marduḷeḍa, to medicines.

ಮದ್ರ್ಳೇ marduḷē, O medicines!

RELATIONSHIP.

ಆಡ್ಳು āḍḷu, (ನಾಕ್ಳು nākḷu) in the plural. In other respects the nouns of the 1st Declension, and those ending in ಇ, or ಎ

ಅಮ್ಮೆ amme, a father.

Plural.

ಅಮ್ಮಾಡ್ಳು ammāḍḷu, fathers.

ಅಮ್ಮಾಡ್ಳೆ ammāḍḷe, of fathers.

ಅಮ್ಮಾಡ್ಳೆಗ್ ammāḍḷegụ, to fathers.

&c. &c.

b., Crude form: ಅಪ್ಪೆ appe, a mother.

	Singular.	Plural.
1. *Nom.*	ಅಪ್ಪೆ appe, a mother.	ಅಪ್ಪೆಅಡ್ಳು appeāḍḷu, mothers.
2. *Gen.*	ಅಪ್ಪೆ appe, of a mother.	ಅಪ್ಪೆಅಡ್ಳೆ appeāḍḷe, of mothers.
3. *Dat.*	ಅಪ್ಪೆಗ್ appegụ, to a mother.	ಅಪ್ಪೆಅಡ್ಳೆಗ್ appeāḍḷegụ, to mothers.
	&c. &c.	&c. &c.

c., Crude form: ಮಗೆ mage, a son.

	Singular.	Plural.
1. *Nom.*	ಮಗೆ mage, a son.	ಮಗಾಡ್ಳು magāḍḷu, sons.
2. *Gen.*	ಮಗ maga, of a son.	ಮಗಾಡ್ಳೆ magāḍḷe, of sons.
3. *Dat.*	ಮಗಕ್ magakụ, to a son.	ಮಗಾಡ್ಳೆಗ್ magāḍḷegụ, to sons.
	&c. &c.	&c. &c

VERBAL NOUNS.

50. Verbal Nouns ending in ಅವು (as, ಮಳ್ಪುನವು malpunavu, doing or the act of doing) have no plural.

	Singular.
1. *Nom.*	ಮಳ್ಪುನವು maḷpunavu, doing, or the act of doing.
2. *Gen.*	ಮಳ್ಪುನೆತ maḷpuneta, of the act of doing.
3. *Dat.*	ಮಳ್ಪುನೆಕ್ maḷpunekụ, to the act of doing.
4. *Accus.*	ಮಳ್ಪುನೆನ್ maḷpunenụ, the act of doing.
5. *Locat.*	ಮಳ್ಪುನೆಟ್ maḷpunetụ, in the act of doing.
6. *Ablat.*	ಮಳ್ಪುನೆಡ್ದ್ maḷpuneḍụdụ, from, by or through the act of doing.
7. *Comm.*	ಮಳ್ಪುನೆಟ maḷpuneṭa, to the act of doing.

2. OF ADJECTIVES.

51. There are very few Simple Adjectives in the Tulu language. This defect is supplied by turning Substantives into Adjectives by affixing to them the participles of the Auxiliary Verbs ಆಪಿನಿ āpini, to become, and ಆದುಪ್ಪುನಿ āduppuni, to be (to have become) and the negative participle ದಾಂತಿ dānti, who, which, and that, have not.

52. Examples of Simple Adjectives: ಪೊಸ posa, new—ಪೊಸ ಕುಂಟು posa kunṭu, a new cloth; ಪೊರ್ಲು porlu, fine—ಪೊರ್ಲು ಬಾಲೆ porlu bāle, a fine child; ಯೆಡ್ಡೆ yeḍḍe, good—ಯೆಡ್ಡೆ ಮಾರ್ಗ yeḍḍe mārga, a good way.

53. Examples of Periphrastic Adjectives: ಬೇನೆ bēne, pain—ಬೇನೆ ಇತ್ತಿ bēne itti, ಬೇನೆ ಉಪ್ಪು bēne uppu, painful; ಬೇನೆ ಉಪ್ಪು ಸಂಕಡ bēne uppu sankaḍa, a painful sickness; ಕತ್ತಲೆ kattale, darkness—ಕತ್ತಲೆ ಇತ್ತಿ kattale itti (or uppu) dark (possessing darkness); ಕತ್ತಲೆ ಇತ್ತಿ ಕೋಣೆ kattale itti (or uppu) kōṇe, a dark room.

54. Negative Adjectives: ಗತಿ ದಾಂತಿ ನರಮಾನಿ gati dānti naramāni, a helpless man.

55. The adjective ಕಿನ್ನಿ kinni, is also used substantively signifying a young; as: ಆನೆದ ಕಿನ್ನಿ āneda kinni, the young of an elephant; ಕೋರಿದ ಕಿನ್ನಿ kōrida kinni, a chicken.

Comparison of Adjectives.

56. There is nothing in Tulu corresponding to the English terminations *er* and *est* (*more* and *most*) by which Adjectives could be compared. Comparison is generally expressed by construing the Adjective with a noun in the Ablative Case; as: ಈ ನರಮಾನ್ಯಡ್ದ್ ಆ ನರಮಾನಿ ಮಲ್ಲಾಯೆ ī naramānyaḍḍdụ ā naramāni mallāye, that man is bigger than this man; ಇಂಬೆ ಮಾತೆರೆಡ್ದ್ ಬುದ್ಧಿವಂತೆ imbe mātereḍḍdụ buddhivante, he is the wisest of all.

57. Comparison may also be expressed by the Dative and Locative Cases. Thus: ಯೆನ ಕುದುರೆಗ್ ನಿನ ಕುದುರೆ ಮಲ್ಲೆ yenakuduregụ nina kudure malle, to my horse your horse (is) a large one, or your horse is larger than mine; ಮಾತ ಕುದುರೆಳೆಡ್ ನಿನ ಕುದುರೆ ಮಲ್ಲೆ māta kudureḷeḍụ nina kudure malle, of, or among all horses your horse (is) a large one, i. e. your horse is the largest of all.

3. OF ADVERBS.

58. Adverbs, like adjectives, are of two kinds: Simple and Periphrastic.

a. Examples of Simple Adverbs; as: ಕೋಡೆ kōḍe, yesterday; ಇನಿ ini, today; ಯೆಲ್ಲೆ yelle, tomorrow; ಕಾಂಡೆ kānḍe, morning; ಬೈಯ baiya, evening; ಪೊಕ್ಕಡೆ pokkaḍe, vainly, in vain; ಸಜ್ಜ sajja, for a time; ಪೆಟ್ಟಿಗೆ peṭṭige, immediately; ಕುಡ kuḍa, again; ಸರ್ತ sarta, straightly; ವೋರೆ wōre, crookedly; ಕಂಕಣೆಮರಂಕಣೆ kankaṇe marankaṇe, ಅಡಿಮೇಲ್ aḍimēlụ, turned upside down, &c.

b. Periphrastic Adverbs are very freely formed by affixing ಆದ್ ādụ, past gerund (of ಆಪಿನಿ āpini) and ದಾಂತೆ dānte (a negative particle) to Substantives and Adjectives; as: ಸಂತೋಷ santōša, gladness—ಸಂತೋಷ ಆದ್ santōša ādụ, gladly; ಪೊಲ್ಲು porlu, beauty—ಪೊಲ್ಲು ಆದ್ porlu ādụ, beautifully; ಸಮಾಧಾನ samādhāna, peace—ಸಮಾಧಾನ ಆದ್ samādhāna ādụ, peacefully; ಗುಟ್ಟು guṭṭu, secret—ಗುಟ್ಟು ಆದ್ guṭṭu ādụ, secretly; ಸರ್ತ sarta, straight—ಸರ್ತ ಆದ್ sarta ādụ, straightly; ಸಮ sama, proper—ಸಮ ಆದ್ sama ādụ, properly; ಗತಿ ದಾಂತೆ gati dānte, helplessly.

59. Some Adverbs are declined like nouns in the singular number.

SECOND SECTION: PRONOUNS.

60. Pronouns, like nouns, are of three kinds. viz: Substantive, Adjective and Adverbial.

1. SUBSTANTIVE PRONOUNS.

61. Substantive Pronouns are either Personal, Reflexive, Demonstrative, Interrogative or Indefinite.

62. A. Personal and Demonstrative Pronouns.

Person.	*Singular.*		*Plural.*	
1st Pers.	ಯಾನ್ yānu̥, I.		ಯೆಂಕುಳು yenkuḷu ನಮ nama } we.	
2nd Pers.	ಈ ī, thou.		ನಿಕುಳು nikuḷu ಈರ್ īru̥ } you.	
3rd Pers.	*Proximate.*	*Remote.*	*Proximate.*	*Remote.*
Masc. *Fem.*	ಇಂಬೆ imbe, he. ಮೋಳ್ mōḷu̥, she.	ಆಯೆ āye, he ಆಳ್ āḷu̥, she	ಮೇರ್ mēru̥ ಮೋಕುಳು mōkuḷu } they.	ಆರ್ āru̥ ಆಕುಳು ākuḷu } they.
Neut.	ಇಂದು indu ಉಂದು undu } this.	ಅವು avu, this.	ಉಂದೆಕುಳು undekuḷu they.	ಐಕುಳು eikuḷu, they.

Remark: 1. The plural "ನಮ nama" of the 1st person has an inclusive meaning; as: ನಮ ಪಾಪಿಷ್ಠೆರ್ ಆದುಳ್ಳ nama pāpiṣṭheru̥ āduḷḷa, we are sinners, i. e. the speaker and the persons spoken to. The plural "ಯೆಂಕುಳು yenkuḷu" has an exclusive meaning; as: ಯೆಂಕುಳು ಪಾಪಿಷ್ಠೆರ್ ಆದುಳ್ಳ yenkuḷu pāpiṣṭheru̥ āduḷḷa, we are sinners; ಆಂಡಲ ಈ, ಓ ದೇವೆರೇ, ಪರಿಶುದ್ಧವಂತೆ ānḍala ī, ō Dēverē, pariśuddhavante, but thou, O God, art holy. ಯೆಂಕುಳು ಕ್ರೈಸ್ತೆರ್, ನಿಕುಳು ಮುಸಲ್ಮಾನೆರ್ yenkuḷu, kreisteru̥ nikuḷu musalmāneru̥, we are Christians, you are Mussulmans, not ನಮ ಕ್ರೈಸ್ತೆರ್, ನಿಕುಳು ಮುಸಲ್ಮಾನೆರ್ nama kreisteru̥ niukḷu musalmāneru̥, because in "ನಮ nama" the other party would be included.

2. The plurals "ಈರ್ īru̥" of the 2nd person, and "ಆರ್ āru̥" of 3rd person are used honorifically when speaking to or of superiors.

63. B. Reflexive Pronouns.

Singular.	*Plural.*
ತಾನ್ tānu̥, himself, herself, itself.	ತನ್‌ಕುಳು tanu̥kuḷu, themselves.

Remark: 1. This Pronoun is used with reference to some other Noun or Pronoun of the third person preceding it.

2. The plural is used honorifically in the second person singular in the sense of "your honor", "your lordship", etc. when speaking to a person of rank.

C. Interrogative Pronouns.

64. ಯೇರ್ yērṳ, who? ದಾನೆ dāne, what? ದಾದವು dādavu, what?

D. Indefinite Pronouns.

65. ಒರಿ wori, one man; ಒರ್ತಿ worti, one woman; ಒಂಜಿ wonji, one thing, etc. ಯೇರ್ಲಾ yērlā, ಯೇರಾಂಡಲಾ yērāṇḍalā, any one.

2. OF ADJECTIVE PRONOUNS.

66. Adjective Pronouns are either Demonstrative, Interrogative or Indefinite.

67. A. Demonstrative.

PROXIMATE.	REMOTE.
ಈ ī, this, these.	ಆ ā, that, those.
ಈತ್ ītṳ, so much.	ಆತ್ ātṳ, so much.
ಇಂಚಿತ್ತಿ inčitti, such.	ಅಂಚಿತ್ತಿ ančitti, such.

B. Interrogative.

68. ವಾ vā, ದಾ dā, ವೊವು vovu which? ಯೇತ್ yētṳ, how much? how many? ಯೆಂಚಿತ್ತಿ yenčitti, what?

C. Indefinite.

69. ಒರಿ wori, ಒರ್ತಿ worti, ಒಂಜಿ wonji, a; ಪಾಕ pāka, some; ಒಂತೆ wonte, little (few), ಮಾತ mäta, all; ಅನೇಕ anēka, many; ದಿಂಜ dinja, plenty; ಬಹಳ bahaḷa, much.

3. ADVERBIAL PRONOUNS.

70. Adverbial Pronouns are either Demonstrative, Interrogative or Indefinite.

71. A. Demonstrative.

PLACE.		TIME.		MODE.	
Proximate.	Remote.	Proximate.	Remote.	Proximate.	Remote.
ಮೂಳು mūḷu, ಮುಳ್ಪ muḷpa — here	ಅವುಳು avuḷu, ಅಳ್ಪ aḷpa — there	ಇನಿ ini — today	ಆನಿ āni — that day	ಇಂಚ inča — thus	ಅಂಚ anča — thus
ಇಡೆ iḍe, ಇಂಚಿ inči — hither	ಅಡೆ aḍe, ಅಂಚಿ anči — thither	ಇತ್ತೆ itte — now	ಆಪಗ āpaga — then	ಇಂಚೆನೆ inčene — so, in this way	ಅಂಚೆನೆ ančene — so, in that way

72. Interrogative.

PLACE.	TIME.	MODE.	CAUSE.
ಓಳು wōḷu, ಒಳ್ಪ woḷpa — where?	ಏಪ yēpa, ಏನಿ yēni — when?	ಎಂಚ yenča — how?	ದಾಯೆ dāye — why?
ಒಡೆ woḍe, ಒಂಚಿ wonči — whither?			

73. C. Indefinite.

PLACE.	TIME.	MODE.
ಒಳಾಂಡಲಾ wōḷānḍalā — wherever.	ಏಪಲಾ yēpalā — always.	ಎಂಚಲಾ yenčalā, ಎಂಚಾಂಡಲಾ yenčānḍalā — anyhow.
ಒರ್ಮೆ worme — everywhere.	ಏಪಾಂಡಲಾ yēpānḍalā — whenever.	ಒಟ್ಟುಗು woṭṭugu — together.
ದುಂಬು dumbu — before, in front.	ಒರ wora, once.	ಬೇಗ bēga, soon.
ಪಿರ, ಪಿರವು pira, piravu — behind.	ಕುಡ kuḍa, again.	ಮೆಲ್ಲ mella, slowly.
ಕೈತಳ್, ಮುಟ್ಟ keitaḷụ, muṭṭa — near, at hand.	ಕಡೇಸ kaḍēsa — late.	ನಿದ್ಪ nidụpa — straightly.
ಮಿತ್ತ್ mittụ — up.	ತೆಂಬುಡ tembuḍa, ತೆಂಬುಡ್ಲಾ tembuḍlā — not yet.	ಸರ್ತ sarta, straightway.
ತಿರ್ತ್ tirtụ — down.		ಒರೆ wōre, crookedly. &c.
ಉಳಯಿ uḷayi — in, inside.		
ಪಿದಯಿ pidayi — out, outside.		
ಸುತ್ತ sutta — around.		
ಸುತ್ತುಮುತ್ತು suttumuttu — roundabout.		

74. Declensions of Pronouns.

	1st PERSON. Singular.	1st PERSON. Plural		2nd PERSON. Singular.	2nd PERSON. Plural.	
1. *Nom.*	ಯಾನ್ yānụ, I.	ನಮ nama, we.	ಯೆಂಕುಳು yenkuḷu, we.	ಈ ī, you or thou.	ಈರ್ īrụ, you.	ನಿಕುಳು nikuḷu, you or ye.
2. *Gen.*	ಯೆನ yena, my.	ನಮ nama, our.	ಯೆಂಕುಳೆ yenkuḷe, our.	ನಿನ nina, your or thine.	ಈರೆ īre, your.	ನಿಕುಳೆ nikuḷe, your.
3. *Dat.*	ಯೆಂಕ್ yenkụ, to me.	ನಂಕ್ nankụ, to us.	ಯೆಂಕುಳೆಗ್ yenku-ḷegụ, to us.	ನಿಕ್ಕ್ nikkụ, to you or to thee.	ಈರೆಗ್ īregụ, to you.	ನಿಕುಳೆಗ್ nikuḷegụ, to you.
4. *Accus.*	ಯೆನನ್ yenanụ, me.	ನಮನ್ namanụ, us.	ಯೆಂಕುಳೆನ್ yenku-ḷenụ, us.	ನಿನನ್ ninanụ, you or thee.	ಈರೆನ್ īrenụ, you.	ನಿಕುಳೆನ್ nikuḷenụ, you.
5. *Locat.*	ಯೆನಡ್ yenaḍụ, in me.	ನಮಡ್ namaḍụ, in us.	ಯೆಂಕುಳೆಡ್ yenku-ḷeḍụ, in us.	ನಿನಡ್ ninaḍụ, in you or in thee.	ಈರೆಡ್ īreḍụ, in you.	ನಿಕುಳೆಡ್ nikuḷeḍụ, in you.
6. *Ablat.*	ಯೆನಡ್ದ್ yenaḍụdụ, from, by or through me.	ನಮಡ್ದ್ namaḍụdụ, from, by or through us.	ಯೆಂಕುಳೆಡ್ದ್ yenku-ḷeḍụdụ, from, by or through us.	ನಿನಡ್ದ್ ninaḍụdụ, from, by or thro-ugh you or thee.	ಈರೆಡ್ದ್ īreḍụdụ, from, by or through you.	ನಿಕುಳೆಡ್ದ್ nikuḷeḍ-ụdụ, from, by or through you.
7. *Comm.*	ಯೆನಡ yenaḍa, to me.	ನಮಡ namaḍa, to us.	ಯೆಂಕುಳೆಡ yenku-ḷeḍa, to us.	ನಿನಡ ninaḍa, to you or to thee.	ಈರೆಡ īreḍa, to you.	ನಿಕುಳೆಡ nikuḷeḍa, to you.
8. *Emph. form.*	ಯಾನೇ yānē, my-self.	ನಮನೇ namanē, ourselves.	ಯೆಂಕುಳೇ yenkuḷē, ourselves.	ಈಯೇ īyē, your-self or thyself.	ಈರೇ īrē, yourself.	ನಿಕುಳೇ nikuḷē, yourselves.

3RD PERSON. (Proximate.)

	MASCULINE.	FEMININE.	MASCULINE AND FEMININE.	NEUTER.	
	Singular.	*Singular.*	*Plural.*	*Singular.*	*Plural.*
1. *No.*	ಇಂಬೆ imbe, he.	ಮೋಳ್ mōḷụ, she.	ಮೋಕುಳು mōkuḷu, they.	ಉಂದು undu, this.	ಉಂದೆಕುಳು undekuḷu, these.
2. *Ge.*	ಇಂಬ್ಯ imbya, his.	ಮೋಳೆ mōḷe, her.	ಮೋಕುಳೆ mōkuḷe, their.	ಉಂದೆತ undeta, of this.	ಉಂದೆಕುಳೆ undekuḷe, of these.
3. *Da.*	ಇಂಬ್ಯಗ್ imbyagụ, to him.	ಮೋಳೆಗ್ mōḷegụ, to her.	ಮೋಕುಳೆಗ್ mōkuḷegụ, to them.	ಉಂದೆಕ್ undekụ, to this.	ಉಂದೆಕುಳೆಗ್ undekuḷegụ, to these.
4. *Acc.*	ಇಂಬ್ಯನ್ imbyanụ, him.	ಮೋಳೆನ್ mōḷenụ, her.	ಮೋಕುಳೆನ್ mōkuḷenụ, them.	ಉಂದೆನ್ undenụ, this.	ಉಂದೆಕುಳೆನ್ undekuḷenụ, these.
5. *Lo.*	ಇಂಬ್ಯಡ್ imbyaḍụ, in him.	ಮೋಳೆಡ್ mōḷeḍụ, in her.	ಮೋಕುಳೆಡ್ mōkuḷeḍụ, in them.	ಉಂದೆಟ್ undeṭụ, in this.	ಉಂದೆಕುಳೆಡ್ undekuḷeḍu, in these.
6. *Ab.*	ಇಂಬ್ಯಡ್ದ್ imbyaḍụḍụ from, by or thro' him.	ಮೋಳೆಡ್ದ್ mōḷeḍụḍụ, from, etc. her.	ಮೋಕುಳೆಡ್ದ್ mōkuḷeḍụḍụ from, etc. them.	ಉಂದೆಡ್ದ್ undeḍụḍụ, from etc. this.	ಉಂದೆಕುಳೆಡ್ದ್ undekuḷeḍụḍụ, from, etc. these.
7. *Co.*	ಇಂಬ್ಯಡ imbyaḍa, to him.	ಮೋಳೆಡ mōḷeḍa, to her.	ಮೋಕುಳೆಡ mōkuḷeḍa, to them.	ಉಂದೆಟ undeṭa, to this.	ಉಂದೆಕುಳೆಡ undekuḷeḍa, to these.
8. *Em. form*	ಇಂಬ್ಯನೇ imbyanē, himself.	ಮೋಳೇ mōḷē, herself.	ಮೋಕುಳೇ mōkuḷē, themselves.	ಉಂದೇ undē, even this.	ಉಂದೆಕುಳೇ undekuḷē, even these.

3rd PERSON. (Remote.)

	MASCULINE.	FEMININE.	MASCULINE AND FEMININE.	NEUTER.	
	Singular.	*Singular.*	*Plural.*	*Singular.*	*Plural.*
1. *Nom.*	ಆಯೆ āye, he.	ಆಳ್ āḷụ, she.	ಆಕುಳು ākuḷu, they.	ಅವು avu, that.	ಐಕುಳು eikuḷu, those.
2. *Gen.*	ಆಯ āya, his.	ಆಳೆ āḷe, her.	ಆಕುಳೆ ākuḷe, their.	ಐತ eita, of that.	ಐಕುಳೆ eikuḷe, of those.
3. *Dat.*	ಆಯಗ್ āyagụ, to him.	ಆಳೆಗ್ āḷegụ, to her.	ಆಕುಳೆಗ್ ākuḷegụ, to them.	ಐಕ್ eikụ, to that.	ಐಕುಳೆಗ್ eikuḷegụ, to those.
4. *Accus.*	ಆಯನ್ āyanụ, him.	ಆಳೆನ್ aḷenụ, her.	ಆಕುಳೆನ್ akuḷenụ, them.	ಐನ್ einụ, that.	ಐಕುಳೆನ್ eikuḷenụ, those.
5. *Locat.*	ಆಯಡ್ āyaḍụ, in him.	ಆಳೆಡ್ āḷeḍụ, in her.	ಆಕುಳೆಡ್ ākuḷeḍụ, in them.	ಐಟ್ eiṭụ, in that.	ಐಕುಳೆಡ್ eikuḷeḍụ, in those.
6. *Ablat.*	ಆಯಡ್ದ್ āyaḍụdụ, from, etc. him.	ಆಳೆಡ್ದ್ āḷeḍụdụ, from, etc. her.	ಆಕುಳೆಡ್ದ್ ākuḷeḍụdụ, from, etc. them.	ಐಡ್ದ್ eiḍụdụ, from, etc. that.	ಐಕುಳೆಡ್ದ್ eikuḷeḍụdụ, from, etc. those.
7. *Comm.*	ಆಯಡ āyaḍa, to him.	ಆಳೆಡ āḷeḍa, to her.	ಆಕುಳೆಡ ākuḷeḍa, to them.	ಐಟ eiṭa, to that.	ಐಕುಳೆಡ eikuḷeḍa, to those.
8. *Emp. form*	ಆಯೆನೇ āyenē, himself.	ಆಳೆನೇ āḷenē, herself.	ಆಕುಳೇ ākuḷē, themselves.	ಅವ್ವೇ avvē, even that.	ಐಕುಳೇ eikuḷē, even those.

Remark: that the remaining Pronouns are inflected according to the above declensions. Thus: ತಾನ್ tanu, like ಯಾನ್ yānu; ಮೇರ್ mēru, ಯೇರ್ yēru, ಆರ್ āru, like ಈರ್ īru; ಇಂಬಳ್ imbaḷu, like ಮೋಳ್ mōḷu; ಇಂದು indu, like ಉಂದು undu; ದಾದವು dādavu, like ಅವು avu.

75. The following Adverbs are only in some cases inflected.

Crude form.	*Genitive.*	*Dative.*	*Ablative.*
ಮೂಳು mūḷu, here.	ಮುಳ್ತ muḷta.		ಮುಳ್ತುಡ್ದು muḷtuḍḍu.
ಅವುಳು avuḷu, there.	ಅಳ್ತ aḷta.		ಅಳ್ತುಡ್ದು aḷtuḍuḍu.
ಓಳು wōḷu, where?	ಒಳ್ತ woḷta.		ಒಳ್ತುಡ್ದು woḷtuḍḍu.
ಒಡೆ woḍe, whence? whither?		ಒಡೆಗ್ woḍegu.	
ಇಡೆ iḍe, hither.		ಇಡೆಗ್ iḍegu.	
ಅಡೆ aḍe, thither.		ಅಡೆಗ್ aḍegu.	
ಇಂಚಿ inči, hitherward.	ಇಂಚಿದ inčida.	ಇಂಚಿಗ್ inčigu.	ಇಂಚಿಡ್ದ್ inčiḍuḍu.
ಅಂಚಿ anči, thitherward.	ಅಂಚಿದ ančida.	ಅಂಚಿಗ್ ančigu.	ಅಂಚಿಡ್ದ್ ančiḍuḍu.
ಒಂಚಿ wonči, whither?	ಒಂಚಿದ vončida.		ಒಂಚಿಡ್ದ್ vončiḍuḍu.
ಇನಿ ini, today.	ಇನಿತ inita.	ಇನಿಕ್ iniku.	ಇನಿಡ್ದ್ iniḍuḍu.
ಕೋಡೆ kōḍe, yesterday.	ಕೋಡೆದ kōḍeda.	ಕೋಡೆಗ್ kōḍegu.	ಕೋಡೆಡ್ದ್ kōḍeḍuḍu.
ಯೆಲ್ಲೆ yelle, tomorrow.	ಯೆಲ್ಲೆದ yelleda.	ಯೆಲ್ಲೆಗ್ yellegu.	ಯೆಲ್ಲೆಡ್ದ್ yelleḍuḍu.
ಯೆಲ್ಲಂಜಿ yellanji, day after tomorrow.	ಯೆಲ್ಲಂಜಿದ yellanjida.	ಯೆಲ್ಲಂಜಿಗ್ yellanjigu.	ಯೆಲ್ಲಂಜಿಡ್ದ್ yellanjiḍuḍu.
ಇತ್ತೆ itte, now.	ಇತ್ತೆದ itteda.	ಇತ್ತೆಗ್ ittegu.	ಇತ್ತೆಡ್ದ್ itteḍuḍu.

THIRD SECTION: NUMERALS.

76. Numerals too are, like Nouns and Pronouns, of three kinds, viz: Substantive, Adjective and Adverbial.

1. SUBSTANTIVE NUMERALS.

77. ಒರಿ **wori**, one (man); ಒತಿೖ **worti**, one (woman); ಒಂಜಿ **wonji**, one (thing).

ಇರ್ವೆರ್ **irverụ**, two (persons).	ಏಳ್ವೆರ್ **yēḷverụ**, seven (persons).
ಮೂವೆರ್ **mūverụ**, three (persons).	ಎಣ್ಮ ಮಂದಿ **yeṇma mande**, eight persons.
ನಾಲ್ವೆರ್ **nālverụ**, four „	ಒಂಬೖ ಮಂದಿ **wormba mande**, nine persons.
ಐವೆರ್ **eiverụ**, five „	ಪತ್ತ್ ಮಂದಿ **pattụ mande**, ten „
ಆಜ್ವೆರ್ **ājverụ**, six „	&c. &c.

Remark: From seven upwards "ಮಂದಿ mande, people" is added to the number.

2. ADJECTIVE NUMERALS.

78. *a.*, Cardinal Numbers.

ಒಂಜಿ **wonji**	೧	1
ರಡ್ಡ್ **raḍḍụ**	೨	2
ಮೂಜಿ **mūji**	೩	3
ನಾಲ್ **nālụ**	೪	4
ಐನ್ **einụ**	೫	5
ಆಜಿ **āji**	೬	6
ಏಳ್ **yēḷụ**	೭	7
ಎಣ್ಮ **yeṇma**	೮	8
ಒಂಬೖ **wormba**	೯	9
ಪತ್ತ್ **pattụ**	೧೦	10
ಪತ್ತೊಂಜಿ **pattonji**	೧೧	11
ಪದ್ರಾಡ್ **padụrāḍụ**	೧೨	12
ಪದ್ ಮೂಜಿ **padụmūji**	೧೩	13
ಪದ್ ನಾಲ್ **padụnālụ**	೧೪	14

ಪದ್ನೈನ್ padụneinụ	೧೫	15
ಪದ್ನಾಜಿ padụnāji	೧೬	16
ಪದ್ನೇಳ್ pādụnēḷụ	೧೭	17
ಪದ್ನೆಣ್ಮ padụneṇma	೧೮	18
ಪದ್ನೊಂರ್ಬ padụnormba	೧೯	19
ಇರ್ವ irva	೨೦	20
ಇರ್ವತೊಂಜಿ irvatonji	೨೧	21
ಇರ್ವತ್ರಡ್ಡ್ irvatụraḍḍụ	೨೨	22
ಇರ್ವತ್ಮೂಜಿ irvatụmūji	೨೩	23
ಇರ್ವತ್ನಾಲ್ irvatụnālụ	೨೪	24
ಇರ್ವತ್ಐನ್ irvatụeinụ, etc.	೨೫	25
ಮುಪ್ಪ muppa.	೩೦	30
ನಾಲ್ಪ nālpa	೪೦	40
ಐವ eiva	೫೦	50
ಅಜಿಪ ajipa	೬೦	60
ಎಳ್ಪ yeḷpa	೭೦	70
ಎಣ್ಪ yeṇpa	೮೦	80
ಸೊಣ್ಪ soṇpa	೯೦	90
ನೂದು nūdu	೧೦೦	100
ನೂತವೊಂಜಿ nūtavonji	೧೦೧	101
ನೂತರಡ್ಡ್ nūtaraḍḍụ	೧೦೨	102
ನೂತಮೂಜಿ nūtamūji, etc.	೧೦೩	103
ನೂತಪತ್ತ್ nūtapattụ, etc.	೧೧೦	110
ನೂತಐವ nūtaeiva, etc.	೧೫೦	150
ಇರ್ನೂದು irnūdu	೨೦೦	200
ಮುನ್ನೂದು munnūdu	೩೦೦	300
ನಾಲ್ನೂದು nālụnūdu (ನಾನೂದು nānūdu)	೪೦೦	400
ಐನೂದು einūdu	೫೦೦	500
ಆಜಿನೂದು ājinūdu	೬೦೦	600
ಏಳ್ನೂದು yēḷụnūdu	೭೦೦	700
ಎಣ್ಮನೂದು yeṇmanūdu	೮೦೦	800
ಒಂರ್ಬನೂದು wormbanūdu	೯೦೦	900

ಸಾರ sāra	೧,೦೦೦	1,000
ಸಾರತವೊಂಜಿ sāratavonji	೧,೦೦೧	1,001
ಸಾರತರಡ್ಡ್ sārataraḍḍu, etc.	೧,೦೦೨	1,002
ಸಾರತಪತ್ತ್ sāratapattu	೧,೦೧೦	1,010
ಸಾರತಇರ್ವ sāratairva	೧,೦೨೦	1,020
ಸಾರತಮುಪ್ಪ sāratamuppa, etc.	೧,೦೩೦	1,030
ಸಾರತನೂದು sāratanūdu	೧,೧೦೦	1,100
ಸಾರತಇರ್ನೂದು sāratairnūdu, etc.	೧,೨೦೦	1,200
ಪತ್ತ್ಸಾರ pattusāra	೧೦,೦೦೦	10,000
ಪತ್ತೊಂಜಿಸಾರ pattonjisāra, etc.	೧೧,೦೦೦	11,000
ಲಕ್ಷ lakša	೧,೦೦,೦೦೦	1,00,000
ಕೋಟಿ kōṭi	೧,೦೦,೦೦,೦೦೦	1,00,00,000

79. *b.*, Ordinal Numbers.

The Ordinal Numbers are formed by adding the affix ಅನೆ ane to the Cardinal Numbers.

ಒಂಜನೆ wonjane	೧ನೆ	1st	ನಾಲನೆ nālane	೪ನೆ	4th
ರಡ್ಡನೆ raḍḍane	೨ನೆ	2nd	ಐನನೆ einane	೫ನೆ	5th
ಮೂಜನೆ mūjane	೩ನೆ	3rd	ಪತ್ತನೆ pattane	೧೦ನೆ	10th
			&c.	&c.	&c.

80. 3. ADVERBIAL NUMERALS.

ಒರ wora, once.
ಇರ್ವೊಳು irvoḷu, twice.
ಮುಕ್ಕೊಳು mukkoḷu, thrice.
ನಲ್ಕೊಳು nalukoḷu, 4 times.
ಐಕೊಳು eikoḷu, or ಐವೊಳು eivoḷu, 5 times.

Remark: This form is only used up to five.

ಒರ್ವಾರ worvāra, once.
ಇರ್ವಾರ irvāra, a second time.
ಮುತ್ತಾರ muttāra, a 3rd time.

Remark: Of this kind these three forms only exist.

ಒಂಜಿ ಸರ್ತಿ wonji sarti, once.
ರಡ್ಡ್ ಸರ್ತಿ raḍḍu sarti, twice.
ಮೂಜಿ ಸರ್ತಿ mūji sarti, 3 times.
&c. &c.

FOURTH SECTION: VERBS.

1. FORMS OF THE VERBS.

81. Tuḷu Verbs have 3 forms: Active, Causative and Reflexive (or middle voice).

82. The Causative is formed by affixing ಆ ā (sometimes ಡು ḍu) to the stem of the present tense of the Active form, as: "ಮಳ್ಪಾ malpā, cause to make" from "ಮಳ್ಪು malpu, to make"; "ನಡಪಾ naḍapā, cause to walk" from "ನಡಪು naḍapu, to walk"; "ನಡಪುಡು cause to walk or to lead" from "ನಡಪು naḍapu, to walk"; "ಕಡಪಾ kaḍapā, cause to cross (a river) or cause to stride through" and "ಕಡಪುಡು kaḍapuḍu, to send" (here the two different affixes imply different meanings); ತರ್ಪಾ tarpā, or ತರ್ಪುಡು tarpuḍu, cause to bring.

83. The Reflexive or middle form is formed by adding ಒಣು woṇu, to the stem of the imperfect tense of the Active or Causative; as: ಮಳ್ತೊಣು maltoṇu, to make for oneself; ತೂವೊಣು tūvoṇu, to see for oneself; ಆಯೆ ತನನ್ ತಾನೇ ಹಾಕೊಂಡೆ āye tananụ tānē hākoṇḍe, he beat himself; ಮಳ್ಪಾವೊಣು malpāvoṇu, cause to make for oneself; ಆಯೆ ತನ್ಕ್ ಒಂಜಿ ತೋಟೊನು ಮಳ್ಪಾವೊಂಡೆ āye tanụkụ wōnji tōṭonu malpāvoṇḍe, he caused to make a garden for himself, i. e. he had a garden made for himself.

Remark: There is no passive form for verbs in Tulu; whenever the passive sense is to be expressed it is done in the following way: ಆಯೆ ಹಾಕ್ಬಿನಾಯೆ ಆಯೆ āye hākụdinạ̄ye āye, he is one who has been beaten, or he has been beaten; ಆಯೆ ನಿಂದಿಸ್ಡಿನಾಯೆ ಆಯೆ āye nindisụdinạ̄ye āye, he is one who was despised, or he was despised.

84. A number of Intransitive Verbs become transitive by changing the terminating letter ಯು yu, into ಪು pu; as:

ಮುಗಿಯು mugiyu, to cease.	ಮುಗಿಪು mugipu, to finish.
ಪರಿಯು pariyu, to tear.	ಪರಿಪು paripu, to tear, to make it tear.
ಉರಿಯು uriyu, to burn.	ಉರಿಪು uripu, to blow.
ಒರಿಯು woriyu, to remain.	ಒರಿಪು woripu, to keep, to preserve.
ನುಡಿಯು nuḍiyu, to sound.	ನುಡಿಪು nuḍipu, to give sound, to speak.

2. TENSES OF THE VERB.

85. There are three principal Tenses, viz: the Present,

Past and Future. Each of the Past and Future Tenses has two forms, Imperfect and Perfect, 1st and 2nd Future.

3. MOODS OF THE VERB.

86. There are six Moods, viz: Indicative, Imperative, Conditional, Infinitive, Potential and Subjunctive, each of which has a positive and negative form.

4. CONJUGATION OF THE VERB.

87. There are two principal conjugations, viz: those in which the participle of the present tense terminates in ಉ u, and those in which it terminates in ಪಿ pi. Each of these two classes has three sub-divisions, the characteristic differences of which appear in the present, past and future tenses of the Indicative, from which all remaining forms may be said to be derived. Accordingly there are 6 conjugations.

88. Compare the following table:—

	Participles.	*Present.*	*Past.*	*Future.*
Participles in ಉ u.	ಮಳ್ಪು maḷpu, making.	ಮಳ್ಪುವೆ maḷpuve, I make.	ಮಳ್ತೆ maḷte, I made.	ಮಳ್ಪೆ maḷpe, I shall make.
	ಕೇಣು kēṇu, hearing.	ಕೇಣುವೆ kēṇuve, I hear.	ಕೇಂಡೆ kēṇḍe, I heard.	ಕೇಣೊಂಬೆ kēṇumbe, I shall hear.
	ಬೂರು būru, falling.	ಬೂರುವೆ būruve, I fall.	ಬೂರಿಯೆ būriye, I fell.	ಬೂರೆ būre, I shall fall.
Participles in ಪಿ pi.	ಸೈಪಿ seipi, dying.	ಸೈಪೆ seipe, I die.	ಸೈತೆ seite, I died.	ಸೈವೆ seive, I shall die.
	ಪಣ್ಪಿ paṇpi, saying.	ಪಣ್ಪೆ paṇpe, I say.	ಪಂಡೆ paṇḍe, I said.	ಪಣೊಂಬೆ paṇumbe, I shall say.
	ಪರ್ಪಿ parpi, drinking.	ಪರ್ಪೆ parpe, I drink.	ಪರಿಯೆ pariye, I drank.	ಪರುವೆ paruve, I shall drink.

89. 1st. Conjugation of Verbs ending in ಪು pu.

Crude form: ಮಳ್ಪು **maḷpu**, make (do).

INDICATIVE MOOD.

PRESENT TENSE.

Singular.

			Positive.	*Negative.*
1st Person.			ಮಳ್ಪುವೆ **maḷpuve**, I make.	ಮಳ್ಪುಜಿ **maḷpuji**, I do not make.
2nd	„		ಮಳ್ಪುವ **muḷpuva**, thou makest.	ಮಳ್ಪುಜ **maḷpuja**, thou doest not make.
3rd	„	*Masc.*	ಮಳ್ಪುವೆ **maḷpuve**, he makes.	ಮಳ್ಪುಜೆ **maḷpuje** he does not make.
„	„	*Fem.*	ಮಳ್ಪುವಳ್ **maḷpuvaḷu̥**, she makes.	ಮಳ್ಪುಜಳ್ **muḷpujaḷu̥**, she does not make.
„	„	*Neut.*	ಮಳ್ಪುಂಡು **muḷpuṇḍu**, it makes.	ಮಳ್ಪುಜಿ **maḷpuji**, it does not make.

Plural.

1st Person.			ಮಳ್ಪುವ **maḷpuva**, we make.	ಮಳ್ಪುಜ **maḷpuja**, we do not make.
2nd	„		ಮಳ್ಪುವರ್ **maḷpuvaru̥**, you make.	ಮಳ್ಪುಜರ್ **maḷpujaru̥**, you do not make.
3rd	„	*Masc.*	ಮಳ್ಪುವೆರ್ **maḷpuveru̥** } they make.	ಮಳ್ಪುಜೆರ್ **maḷpujeru̥** } they do not make.
„	„	*Fem.*	ಮಳ್ಪುವೆರ್ **maḷpuveru̥** } they make.	ಮಳ್ಪುಜೆರ್ **maḷpujeru̥** } they do not make.
„	„	*Neut.*	ಮಳ್ಪುವ **maḷpuva** } they make.	ಮಳ್ಪುಜ **maḷpuja** } they do not make.

Remark: Though the first person singular in all tenses is spelt like the 3rd person masculine, they are pronounced differently; the terminating ೆ e, in the former sounding nearly like 'a' in man (ಮಳ್ಪುವೆ malpuve), that in the latter like 'e' in men (ಮಳ್ಪುವೆ malpuve).

PAST TENSE.

IMPERFECT.

Singular.

			Positive.	*Negative.*
1st Person.			ಮಳ್ತೆ maḷte, I made.	ಮಳ್ತಿಜಿ maḷtiji, I did not make.
2nd	„		ಮಳ್ತ maḷta, thou madest.	ಮಳ್ತಿಜ maḷtija, thou didst not make.
3rd	„	*Masc.*	ಮಳ್ತೆ maḷte, he made.	ಮಳ್ತಿಜೆ maḷtije, he did not make.
„	„	*Fem.*	ಮಳ್ತಳ್ maḷtaḷu, she made.	ಮಳ್ತಿಜಳ್ maḷtijaḷu, she did not make.
„	„	*Neut.*	ಮಳ್ತ್ಂಡ್ maḷtuṇḍu, it made.	ಮಳ್ತಿಜಿ maḷtiji, it did not make.

Plural.

1st Person.			ಮಳ್ತ maḷta, we made.	ಮಳ್ತಿಜ maḷtija, we did not make.
2nd	„		ಮಳ್ತರ್ maḷtaru, you made.	ಮಳ್ತಿಜರ್ maḷtijaru, you did not make.
3rd	„	*Masc.*	ಮಳ್ತೆರ್ maḷteru } they made.	ಮಳ್ತಿಜೆರ್ maḷtijeru } they did not make.
„	„	*Fem.*	ಮಳ್ತೆರ್ maḷteru } they made.	ಮಳ್ತಿಜೆರ್ maḷtijeru } they did not make.
„	„	*Neut.*	ಮಳ್ತ maḷta } they made.	ಮಳ್ತಿಜ maḷtija } they did not make.

Remark: All verbs with ಪ್ಪು ppu, in the root, as ಲಪ್ಪುನಿ lappuni, ದೆಪ್ಪುನಿ deppuni, have ತ್ತೆ tte, in the imperfect tense; as: ಲತ್ತೆ latte, ದೆತ್ತೆ dette, etc.

PERFECT TENSE.

Singular.

			Positive.	Negative.
1st Person.			ಮಳ್ತ್ದೆ maḷtuḍe, I have made.	ಮಳ್ತ್ದಿಜಿ maḷtuḍiji, I have not made.
2nd	„		ಮಳ್ತ್ದ maḷtuḍa, thou hast made.	ಮಳ್ತ್ದಿಜ maḷtuḍija, thou hast not made.
3rd	„	*Masc.*	ಮಳ್ತ್ದೆ maḷtuḍe, he has made.	ಮಳ್ತ್ದಿಜೆ maḷtuḍije, he has not made.
„	„	*Fem.*	ಮಳ್ತ್ದಳ್ maḷtuḍaḷu, she has made.	ಮಳ್ತ್ದಿಜಳ್ maḷtuḍijaḷu, she has not made.
„	„	*Neut.*	ಮಳ್ತ್ದ್ಂಡ್ maḷtuḍuṇḍu, it has made.	ಮಳ್ತ್ದಿಜಿ maḷtuḍiji, it has not made.

Plural.

1st Person.			ಮಳ್ತ್ದ maḷtuḍa, we have made.	ಮಳ್ತ್ದಿಜ maḷtuḍija, we have not made.
2nd	„		ಮಳ್ತ್ದರ್ maḷtuḍaru, you have made.	ಮಳ್ತ್ದಿಜರ್ maḷtuḍijaru, you have not made.
3rd	„	*Masc.*	ಮಳ್ತ್ದೆರ್ maḷtuḍeru	ಮಳ್ತ್ದಿಜೆರ್ maḷtuḍijeru
„	„	*Fem.*	ಮಳ್ತ್ದೆರ್ maḷtuḍeru } they have made.	ಮಳ್ತ್ದಿಜೆರ್ maḷtuḍijeru } they have not made.
„	„	*Neut.*	ಮಳ್ತ್ದ maḷtuḍa	ಮಳ್ತ್ದಿಜ maḷtuḍija

PLUPERFECT TENSE.

(ಮಳ್ತ್ದ್ maḷtụdụ, *Gerund Perfcet* and ಇತ್ತೆ itte, *Imperfect tense* of ಉಪ್ಪುನಿ uppuni, to be.)

Singular.

		Positive.	Negative.
1st Person.		ಮಳ್ತ್ದಿತ್ತೆ maḷtụditte, I had made.	ಮಳ್ತ್ದಿತ್ತ್ಜಿ maḷtụdittụji, I had not made.
2nd „		ಮಳ್ತ್ದಿತ್ತ maḷtụditta, thou hadst made.	ಮಳ್ತ್ದಿತ್ತ್ಜ maḷtụdittụja, thou hadst not made.
3rd „	*Masc.*	ಮಳ್ತ್ದಿತ್ತೆ maḷtụditte, he had made.	ಮಳ್ತ್ದಿತ್ತ್ಜೆ maḷtụdittụje, he had not made.
„ „	*Fem.*	ಮಳ್ತ್ದಿತ್ತಳ್ maḷtụdittaḷụ, she had made.	ಮಳ್ತ್ದಿತ್ತ್ಜಳ್ muḷtụdittụjaḷụ, she had not made.
„ „	*Neut.*	ಮಳ್ತ್ದಿತ್ತ್ಂಡ್ maḷtụdittụṇḍụ, it had made.	ಮಳ್ತ್ದಿತ್ತ್ಜ maḷtụdittụja, it had not made.

Plural.

		Positive.	Negative.
1st Person.		ಮಳ್ತ್ದಿತ್ತ maḷtụditta, we had made.	ಮಳ್ತ್ದಿತ್ತ್ಜ maḷtụdittụja, we had not made.
2nd „		ಮಳ್ತ್ದಿತ್ತರ್ maḷtụdittarụ, you had made.	ಮಳ್ತ್ದಿತ್ತ್ಜರ್ maḷtụdittụjarụ, you had not made.
3rd „	*Masc.*	ಮಳ್ತ್ದಿತ್ತೆರ್ maḷtụditterụ } they had made.	ಮಳ್ತ್ದಿತ್ತ್ಜೆರ್ maḷtụdittụjerụ } they had not made.
„ „	*Fem.*	ಮಳ್ತ್ದಿತ್ತೆರ್ maḷtụditterụ } they had made.	ಮಳ್ತ್ದಿತ್ತ್ಜೆರ್ maḷtụdittụjerụ } they had not made.
„ „	*Neut.*	ಮಳ್ತ್ದಿತ್ತ maḷtụditta } they had made.	ಮಳ್ತ್ದಿತ್ತ್ಜ maḷtụdittụja } they had not made.

FUTURE TENSE.

1st FUTURE.

Singular.

			Positive.	*Negative.*
1st Person.			ಮಳ್ಪೆ **maḷpe,** I shall make.	ಮಳ್ಪಯೆ **maḷpaye,** I shall not make.
2nd	„		ಮಳ್ಪ **maḷpa,** thou wilt make.	ಮಳ್ಪಯ **maḷpaya,** thou wilt not make.
3rd	„	*Masc.*	ಮಳ್ಪೆ **maḷpe,** he will make.	ಮಳ್ಪಯೆ **maḷpaye,** he will not make.
„	„	*Fem.*	ಮಳ್ಪಳ್ **maḷpaḷụ,** she will make.	ಮಳ್ಪಯಳ್ **maḷpayaḷụ,** she will not make.
„	„	*Neut.*	ಮಳ್ಪು **maḷpu,** it will make.	ಮಳ್ಪಂದ್ **maḷpandụ,** it will not make.

Plural.

1st Person.			ಮಳ್ಪ **maḷpa,** we shall make.	ಮಳ್ಪಯ **maḷpaya,** we shall not make.
2nd	„		ಮಳ್ಪರ್ **maḷparụ,** you will make.	ಮಳ್ಪಯರ್ **maḷpayarụ,** you will not make.
3rd	„	*Masc.*	ಮಳ್ಪೆರ್ **maḷperụ** } they will make.	ಮಳ್ಪಯೆರ್ **maḷpayerụ** } they will not make.
„	„	*Fem.*	ಮಳ್ಪೆರ್ **maḷperụ** } they will make.	ಮಳ್ಪಯೆರ್ **maḷpayerụ** } they will not make.
„	„	*Neut.*	ಮಳ್ಪ **maḷpa** } they will make.	ಮಳ್ಪಯ **maḷpaya** } they will not make.

2nd **FUTURE** (Future Perfect Tense).

(ಮಳ್ತ್ದ್ **maḷtụdụ**, *Gerund Perfect* and ಉಪ್ಪೆ **uppe**, etc. *Future Tense* of ಉಪ್ಪುನಿ **uppuni**, to be.)

Singular.

	Positive.	*Negative.*
1st Person.	ಮಳ್ತ್ದುಪ್ಪೆ **maḷtụduppe**, I shall have made.	ಮಳ್ತ್ದುಪ್ಪಯೆ **maḷtụduppaye**, I shall not have made.
2nd „	ಮಳ್ತ್ದುಪ್ಪ **maḷtụduppa**, thou wilt have made.	ಮಳ್ತ್ದುಪ್ಪಯ **maḷtụduppaya**, thou wilt not have made.
3rd „ *Masc.*	ಮಳ್ತ್ದುಪ್ಪೆ **maḷtụduppe**, he will have made.	ಮಳ್ತ್ದುಪ್ಪಯೆ **maḷtụduppaye**, he will not have made.
„ „ *Fem.*	ಮಳ್ತ್ದುಪ್ಪಳ್ **maḷtụduppaḷụ**, she will have made.	ಮಳ್ತ್ದುಪ್ಪಯಳ್ **maḷtụduppayaḷụ**, she will not have made.
„ „ *Neut.*	ಮಳ್ತ್ದುಪ್ಪು **maḷtụduppu**, it will have made.	ಮಳ್ತ್ದುಪ್ಪಂದ್ **maḷtụduppandụ**, it will not have made.

Plural.

1st Person.	ಮಳ್ತ್ದುಪ್ಪ **maḷtụduppa**, we shall have made.	ಮಳ್ತ್ದುಪ್ಪಯ **maḷtụduppaya**, we shall not have made.
2nd „	ಮಳ್ತ್ದುಪ್ಪರ್ **maḷtụdupparụ**, you will have made.	ಮಳ್ತ್ದುಪ್ಪಯರ್ **maḷtụduppayarụ**, you will not have made.
3rd „ *Masc.*	ಮಳ್ತ್ದುಪ್ಪೆರ್ **maḷtụdupperụ** } they will have made.	ಮಳ್ತ್ದುಪ್ಪಯೆರ್ **maḷtụduppayerụ** } they will not have made.
„ „ *Fem.*	ಮಳ್ತ್ದುಪ್ಪೆರ್ **maḷtụdupperụ** } they will have made.	ಮಳ್ತ್ದುಪ್ಪಯೆರ್ **maḷtụduppayerụ** } they will not have made.
„ „ *Neut.*	ಮಳ್ತ್ದುಪ್ಪ **maḷtụduppa** } they will have made.	ಮಳ್ತ್ದುಪ್ಪಯ **maḷtụduppaya** } they will not have made.

IMPERATIVE MOOD.

Singular.

	Positive.	*Negative.*
1st Person.	ಮಳ್ಪುಗೆ **maḷpuge,** let me make; I will make.	ಮಳ್ಪಂದೆ ಉಪ್ಪುಗೆ **maḷpande uppuge,** let me not make; I will not make.
2nd „	ಮಳ್ಪುಲ **maḷpula,** make, or do thou make.	ಮಳ್ಪಡ **maḷpaḍa,** ಮಳ್ಪಂದೆ ಉಪ್ಪುಲ **maḷpande uppula,** do not make.
3rd „	ಮಳ್ಪಡ್ **maḷpaḍụ,** let him, her or it make.	ಮಳ್ಪಂದೆ ಉಪ್ಪಡ್ **maḷpande uppaḍụ,** let him, her, or it not make.

Plural.

1st Person.	ಮಳ್ಪುಗ **maḷpuga** let us make.	ಮಳ್ಪಂದೆ ಉಪ್ಪುಗ **maḷpande uppuga,** let us not make.
2nd „	ಮಳ್ಪುಲೆ **maḷpule,** make you, or do you make.	ಮಳ್ಪಡೆ **maḷpaḍe,** ಮಳ್ಪಂದೆ ಉಪ್ಪುಲೆ **maḷpande uppule,** do not make.
3rd „	ಮಳ್ಪಡ್ **maḷpaḍụ,** let them make.	ಮಳ್ಪಂದೆ ಉಪ್ಪಡ್ **maḷpande uppaḍụ,** let them not make.

CONDITIONAL MOOD.

Singular.

		Positive.	*Negative.*
1st Person.		ಮಳ್ತ್ದ್ವೆ maḷtụdve, I should make.	ಮಳ್ತ್ದ್ವಯೆ maḷtụdvaye, I should not make.
2nd „		ಮಳ್ತ್ದ್ವ maḷtụdva, thou wouldst make.	ಮಳ್ತ್ದ್ವಯ maḷtụdvaya, thou wouldst not make.
3rd „	*Masc.*	ಮಳ್ತ್ದ್ವೆ maḷtụdve, he would make.	ಮಳ್ತ್ದ್ವಯೆ maḷtụdvaye, he would not make.
„ „	*Fem.*	ಮಳ್ತ್ದ್ವಳ್ maḷtụdvaḷụ, she would make.	ಮಳ್ತ್ದ್ವಯಳ್ maḷtụdvayaḷụ, she would not make.
„ „	*Neut.*	ಮಳ್ತ್ದು maḷtụdu, it would make.	ಮಳ್ತ್ದ್ವಂದ್ maḷtụdvandụ, it would not make.

Plural.

		Positive.	*Negative.*
1st Person.		ಮಳ್ತ್ದ್ವ maḷtụdva, we should make.	ಮಳ್ತ್ದ್ವಯ maḷtụdvaya, we should not make.
2nd „		ಮಳ್ತ್ದ್ವರ್ maḷtụdvarụ, you would make.	ಮಳ್ತ್ದ್ವಯರ್ maḷtụdvayarụ, you would not make.
3rd „	*Masc.*	ಮಳ್ತ್ದ್ವೆರ್ maḷtụdverụ } they would make.	ಮಳ್ತ್ದ್ವಯೆರ್ maḷtụdvayerụ } they would not make.
„ „	*Fem.*	ಮಳ್ತ್ದ್ವೆರ್ maḷtụdverụ } they would make.	ಮಳ್ತ್ದ್ವಯೆರ್ maḷtụdvayerụ } they would not make.
„ „	*Neut.*	ಮಳ್ತ್ದ್ವ maḷtụdva } they would make.	ಮಳ್ತ್ದ್ವಯ maḷtụdvaya } they would not make.

Remark: The Conditional has the form of the Future Tense, but is used in all other tenses too.

INFINITIVE MOOD.

PRESENT TENSE.

1st *Infinitive.*

Positive.	*Negative.*
ಮಳ್ಪುನಿ **malpuni** (ಮಳ್ಪುನೇ **malpunē**), (to) make.	ಮಳ್ಪಂದೆ ಉಪ್ಪುನಿ **malpande uppuni,** not (to) make.

PAST TENSE.

IMPERFECT AND PERFECT.

ಮಳ್ತಿನಿ **maltini** (ಮಳ್ತಿನೇ **maltinē**), (to) have made. ಮಳ್ತ್ದಿನಿ **maltudini** (ಮಳ್ತ್ದಿನೇ **maltudinē**), (to) have had made.	ಮಳ್ಪಂದೆ ಇತ್ತಿನಿ **malpande ittini,** not (to) have made.

Remark: 1. This Infinitive is frequently used instead of the personal forms of the Verb; as: ದಾನೆ ಬತ್ತಿನಿ dāne battini, why didst thou come? ದಾನೆ ಬತ್ತರ್ dāne battaru, why did you come? ಆಯೆ ಈ ಪ್ರಕಾರ ಮಳ್ತಿನಿ āye ī prakāra maltini, (instead of ಆಯೆ ಈ ಪ್ರಕಾರ ಮಳ್ತೆ āye ī prakāra malte), he has done in this way; ಆಕುಲು ಈ ಪ್ರಕಾರ ಪಣ್ಪಿನಿ ākulu ī prakāra panpini (instead of ಆಕುಲು ಈ ಪ್ರಕಾರ ಪಣ್ಪೆರ್ ākulu ī prakāra panperu), they say so.

2. The form "ಮಳ್ಪುನೇ malpunē" expresses emphasis; as: ಆಯೆ ಬರ್ಪಿನೇ ಇಜ್ಜಿ āye barpinē ijji, he does not come anyhow; ನಿಕುಲು ಬುಡ್ಪಿನೇ ಇಜ್ಜಿ nikulu budpinē ijji, you do not leave anyhow.

2nd *Infinitive* (*Supine*).

ಮಳ್ಪೆರೆ **malpere,** to make.	ಮಳ್ಪಂದೆ ಉಪ್ಪೆರೆ **malpande uppere,** not to make.

ಆ ಬೇಲೆ ಮಳ್ಪೆರೆ ಬತ್ತೆ **ā bēle malpere batte,** I came to do that work.

GERUNDS AND PARTICIPLES.

PRESENT AND FUTURE.

	Positive.	*Negative.*
Ger.	ಮಳ್ತೊಣ್ಡು **maḷtoṇḍu**, making.	ಮಳ್ಪಂದೆ **maḷpande**, not making.
Part.	ಮಳ್ಪ್ಪ **maḷpu**, making or that is making.	ಮಳ್ಪಂದಿ **maḷpandi**, not making or that is not making.

PAST TENSE.

IMPERFECT.

Part.	ಮಳ್ತಿ **maḷti**, made, that made or that is made.	ಮಳ್ಪಂದಿ **maḷpandi**, not made, that had or is not made.

PERFECT.

Ger.	ಮಳ್ತ್ದ್ **maḷtuḍu**, having made.	ಮಳ್ಪಂದೆ **maḷpande**, having not made.
Part.	ಮಳ್ತ್ದಿ **maḷtuḍi**, having made or being made, that has made or that has been made.	ಮಳ್ಪಂದಿ **maḷpandi**, having or being not made, that has not, or has not been made.

PARTICIPIAL AND VERBAL NOUNS.

PRESENT AND FUTURE.

Singular.

Masc.	ಮಳ್ಪುನಾಯೆ **maḷpunāye**, maker, he that makes.	ಮಳ್ಪಂದಿನಾಯೆ **maḷpandināye**, he that does not make.
Fem.	ಮಳ್ಪುನಾಳ್ **maḷpunāḷu** she that makes.	ಮಳ್ಪಂದಿನಾಳ್ **maḷpandināḷu**, she that does not make.
Neut.	ಮಳ್ಪುನವು **maḷpunavu**, that which makes; or more frequently: the act of making.	ಮಳ್ಪಂದಿನವು **maḷpandinavu**, that which does not make.

Plural.

	Positive.		*Negative.*	
Masc. & fem.	ಮಳ್ಪುನಾಕುಳು maḷpunākuḷu	those that make.	ಮಳ್ಪಂದಿನಾಕುಳು maḷpandinākuḷu	those that do not make.
Neut.	ಮಳ್ಪುನೈಕುಳು maḷpuneikuḷu		ಮಳ್ಪಂದಿನೈಕುಳು maḷpandineikuḷu	

PAST TENSE.

IMPERFECT.

Singular.

ಮಳ್ತಿನಾಯೆ maḷtināye he that made. &c.	As in the present tense.

Plural.

ಮಳ್ತಿನಾಕುಳು maḷtinākuḷu, those that made. &c.	Do.

PERFECT.

Singular.

ಮಳ್ತುದಿನಾಯೆ maḷtụdināye, he that has made. &c.	Do.

Plural.

ಮಳ್ತುದಿನಾಕುಳು maḷtụdinākuḷu, those that have made. &c.	Do.

Remark: 1. By adding the adverbial particle 'ಅಗ aga' to the root of the Verb, the *time at which the action takes* place is expressed; as: (ಮಳ್ಪು malpu+ನ್ n+ಅಗ aga) ಮಳ್ಪುನಗ malpunaga, when making; ಆಯಿ ಒಣಸ್ ಮಳ್ಪುನಗ āye woṇasu malpunaga, when he takes his dinner.

2. In the same way by adding the particle "ಎಂಗೆ enge" to the root of the Verb, the *point of time* at which the action terminates is expressed; as: (ಮಳ್ಪು malpu+ನ್ n+ಎಂಗೆ enge) ಮಳ್ಪುನೆಂಗೆ malpunenge, till making; ಯಾನ್ ಉಂಡೆನ್ ಮಳ್ಪುನೆಂಗೆ yānu undenu malpunenge, till I make this.

3. The Subjunctive Mood is formed by adding the particle "ಡ ḍa, if" to the forms of the verb in all tenses; as: ಮಳ್ಪುವೆಡ malpuveḍa, if I make; ಮಳ್ಪುವಡ malpuvaḍa, if thou make (st); ಮಳ್ತೆಡ malteḍa, if I made etc. See the following table.

SUBJUNCTIVE MOOD.

PRESENT TENSE.

Singular.

			Positive.	*Negative.*
1st Person.			ಮಳ್ಪುವೆಡ malpuveḍa, if I make.	ಮಳ್ಪುಜೆಡ malpujeḍa, if I do not make.
2nd	„		ಮಳ್ಪುವಡ malpuvaḍa, if thou make (st.)	ಮಳ್ಪುಜಡ malpujaḍa, if thou do (est) not make.
3rd	„	*Masc.*	ಮಳ್ಪುವೆಡ malpuveḍa, if he make (s.)	ಮಳ್ಪುಜೆಡ malpujeḍa, if he do (es) not make.
„	„	*Fem.*	ಮಳ್ಪುವಳ್ಡ malpuvaḷuḍa, if she make (s.)	ಮಳ್ಪುಜಳ್ಡ malpujaḷuḍa, if she do (es) not make.
„	„	*Neut.*	ಮಳ್ಪುಂಡ malpunḍa (ಮಳ್ಪುಂಡುಡ malpunḍuḍa), if it make (s.)	ಮಳ್ಪುಜಿಡ malpujiḍa, if it do (es) not make.

Plural.

		Positive.	*Negative.*
1st Person.		ಮಳ್ಪುವಡ **maḷpuvaḍa,** if we make.	ಮಳ್ಪುಜಡ **maḷpujaḍa,** if we do not make.
2nd „		ಮಳ್ಪುವರ್ಡ **maḷpuvarḍa,** if you make.	ಮಳ್ಪುಜರ್ಡ **maḷpujarḍa,** if you do not make.
3rd „	*Masc.*	ಮಳ್ಪುವೆರ್ಡ **maḷpuverḍa**	ಮಳ್ಪುಜೆರ್ಡ **maḷpujerḍa**
„ „	*Fem.*	ಮಳ್ಪುವೆರ್ಡ **maḷpuverḍa** } if they make.	ಮಳ್ಪುಜೆರ್ಡ **maḷpujerḍa** } if they do not make.
„ „	*Neut.*	ಮಳ್ಪುವಡ **maḷpuvaḍa**	ಮಳ್ಪುಜಡ **maḷpujaḍa**

PAST TENSE.

Singular.

1st Person.	ಮಳ್ತೆಡ **maḷteḍa,** if I made.	ಮಳ್ತಿಜಿಡ **maḷtijiḍa,** if I did not make.
2nd „	ಮಳ್ತಡ **maḷtaḍa,** if thou made (st).	ಮಳ್ತಿಜಡ **maḷtijaḍa,** if thou did (st) not make.
	&c.	&c.

Plural.

1st Person.	ಮಳ್ತಡ **maḷtaḍa,** if we made.	ಮಳ್ತಿಜಡ **maḷtijaḍa,** if we did not make.
2nd „	ಮಳ್ತರ್ಡ **maḷtarḍa,** if you made.	ಮಳ್ತಿಜರ್ಡ **maḷtijarḍa,** if you did not make.
	&c.	&c.

POTENTIAL MOOD.

Positive.	*Negative.*
ಮಳ್ಪೊಲಿ malpoli (ಮಳ್ಪ malpu+ಒಲಿ oli), I &c. may make.	ಮಳ್ಪೆರೆ ಬಲ್ಲಿ malpere balli, I &c. may not make.
ಮಳ್ಪೊಡು malpoḍu (ಮಳ್ಪ malpu+ಬೋಡು bōḍu) I &c. must or need make.	ಮಳ್ಪೊಡ್ಚಿ malpoḍči (ಮಳ್ಪ malpu+ಬೋಡು bōḍu+ಇಜ್ಜಿ ijji), I &c. must not or need not make.
ಮಳ್ಪೆರೆ malpere { ತೀರುಂಡು tīrunḍu / ತೆರಿಯುಂಡು teriyunḍu / ಕೂಡುಂಡು kūḍunḍu } I &c. can make or know (how) to make.	ಮಳ್ಪೆರೆ malpere { ಬಲ್ಲಿ balli / ತೆರಿಯುಜಿ teryuji / ಕೂಡುಜಿ kūḍuji } I &c. cannot make or know not (how) to make.

CONTINUED FORM.

ಮಳ್ತೊಣ್ಡು ಉಪ್ಪುನಿ maltoṇdu uppuni, to be making.

This form is obtained by adding to the *Present Gerund* "ಮಳ್ತೊಣ್ಡು maltoṇḍu," the auxiliary verb "ಉಪ್ಪುನಿ uppuni (or ಆದುಪ್ಪುನಿ āduppuni), to be," and inflecting it; as:

PRESENT TENSE.

Singular.

Positive.	*Negative.*
1st Person. ಮಳ್ತೊಣ್ದುಪ್ಪುವೆ (or—ಉಳ್ಳೆ) **maḷtoṇḍuppuve** (or —**uḷḷe**), I am amking.	ಮಳ್ತೊಣ್ದುಪ್ಪುಜಿ **maḷtoṇḍuppuji**, I am not making.
&c. &c.	&c. &c.

Plural.

1st Person. ಮಳ್ತೊಣ್ದುಪ್ಪುವ (or—ಉಳ್ಳ) **maḷtoṇḍuppuva** (or —**uḷḷa**), we are making.	ಮಳ್ತೊಣ್ದುಪ್ಪುಜ **maḷtoṇḍuppuja**, we are not making.
&c. &c.	&c. &c.

FREQUENTATIVE FORM.

Frequency of action is expressed by inserting ಪೇ, between the stem of the present tense and the affixes of the Verb; as:

PRESENT AND FUTURE TENSES.

Singular.	*Plural.*
1st Person. ಮಳ್ಪೇವೆ **maḷpēve**, I make again and again.	ಮಳ್ಪೇವ **maḷpēva**, we make again and again.
&c. &c.	&c. &c.

PAST TENSE.

1st Person. ಮಳ್ಪೇದೆ **maḷpēde**, I made again and again.	ಮಳ್ಪೇದ **maḷpēda**, we made again and again.
&c. &c.	&c. &c.

INTENSIVE FORM.

Present tense.	*Past tense.*
ಮಳ್ತ್ರುವೆ **maḷtruve**, I make energetically.	ಮಳ್ತ್ರಿಯೆ **maḷtriye**, I made energetically.
&c.	&c.

90. 2nd Conjugation of Verbs ending in ಣು **ṇu.**

Crude form: ಕೇಣು **kēṇu**, hear.

INDICATIVE MOOD.

PRESENT TENSE.

Singular.

	Positive.	*Negative.*
1st Person.	ಕೇಣುವೆ **kēṇuve**, I hear.	ಕೇಣುಜಿ **kēṇuji**, I do not hear.
2nd "	ಕೇಣುವ **kēṇuva**, thou hearest.	ಕೇಣುಜ **kēṇuja**, thou doest not hear.
	&c.	&c.

Plural.

1st Person.	ಕೇಣುವ **kēṇuva**, we hear.	ಕೇಣುಜ **kēṇuja**, we do not hear.
2nd "	ಕೇಣುವರ್ **kēṇuvaru**, you hear.	ಕೇಣುಜರ್ **kēṇujaru**, you do not hear.
	&c.	&c.

PAST TENSE.

IMPERFECT.

Singular.

	Positive.	*Negative*
1st Person.	ಕೇಂಡೆ **kēṇḍe,** I heard.	ಕೇಂಡ್ಜಿ **kēṇḍuji,** I did not hear.
2nd „	ಕೇಂಡ **kēṇḍa,** thou heardst.	ಕೇಂಡ್ಜ **kēṇḍuja,** thou didst not hear.
	&c.	&c.

Plural.

1st Person.	ಕೇಂಡ **kēṇḍa,** we heard.	ಕೇಂಡ್ಜ **kēṇḍuja,** we did not hear.
2nd „	ಕೇಂಡರ್ **kēṇḍaru,** you heard.	ಕೇಂಡ್ಜರ್ **kēṇḍujaru,** you did not hear.
	&c.	&c.

PERFECT.

Singular.

1st Person.	ಕೇಣ್ದೆ **kēṇuḍe,** I have heard.	ಕೇಣ್ದಿಜಿ **kēṇuḍiji,** I have not heard.
2nd „	ಕೇಣ್ದ **kēṇuḍa,** thou hast heard.	ಕೇಣ್ದಿಜ **kēṇuḍija,** thou hast not heard.
	&c.	&c.

Plural.

	Positive.	*Negative.*
1st Person.	ಕೇಣ್ದ **kēṇụda**, we have heard.	ಕೇಣ್ದಿಜ **kēṇụdija**, we have not heard.
2nd „	ಕೇಣ್ದರ್ **keṇụdarụ**, you have heard.	ಕೇಣ್ದಿಜರ್ **kēṇụdijarụ**, you have not heard.
	&c.	&c.

PLUPERFECT TENSE.

Singular.

1st Person.	ಕೇಣ್ದಿತ್ತೆ **kēṇụditte**, I had heard.	ಕೇಣ್ದಿತ್ತುಜಿ **kēṇụdittụji**, I had not heard.
2nd „	ಕೇಣ್ದಿತ್ತ **keṇụditta**, thou hadst heard.	ಕೇಣ್ದಿತ್ತುಜ **kēṇụdittụja**, thou hadst not heard.
	&c.	&c.

Plural.

1st Person.	ಕೇಣ್ದಿತ್ತ **kēṇụditta**, we had heard.	ಕೇಣ್ದಿತ್ತುಜ **kēṇụdittụja**, we had not heard.
2nd „	ಕೇಣ್ದಿತ್ತರ್ **kēṇụdittarụ**, you had heard.	ಕೇಣ್ದಿತ್ತುಜರ್ **kēṇụdittụjarụ**, you had not heard.
	&c.	&c.

FUTURE TENSE.

1st FUTURE.

Singular.

	Positive.	*Negative.*
1st Person.	ಕೇಣ್ಂಬೆ **kēṇuṃbe** (seldom: ಕೇಣೆ **kēṇē**), I shall hear.	ಕೇಣಾಯೆ **kēṇaye**, I shall not hear.
2nd „	ಕೇಣ್ಂಬ **kēṇuṃba** (seldom: ಕೇಣ **kēṇa**), thou wilt hear.	ಕೇಣಾಯ **kēṇaya**, thou wilt not hear.
	&c.	&c.

Plural.

1st Person.	ಕೇಣ್ಂಬ **kēṇuṃba**, we shall hear.	ಕೇಣಾಯ **kēṇaya**, we shall not hear.
2nd „	ಕೇಣ್ಂಬರ್ **kēṇuṃbaru**, you will hear.	ಕೇಣಾಯರ್ **kēṇayaru**, you will not hear.
	&c.	&c.

2nd FUTURE (FUTURE PERFECT).

(ಕೇಂಡ್ದ್ **kēṇḍuḍu**, *Gerund Perfect* and ಉಪ್ಪೆ **uppe**, etc. *Future tense* of ಉಪ್ಪುನಿ **uppuni.**)

Singular.

1st Person.	ಕೇಂಡ್ದುಪ್ಪೆ **kēṇḍuḍuppe**, I shall have heard.	ಕೇಂಡ್ದುಪ್ಪಯೆ **kēṇḍuḍuppaye**, I shall not have heard.
2nd „	ಕೇಂಡ್ದುಪ್ಪ **kēṇḍuḍuppa**, thou wilt have heard.	ಕೇಂಡ್ದುಪ್ಪಯ **kēṇḍuḍuppaya**, thou wilt not have heard.
	&c.	&c.

Plural.

	Positive.	Negative.
1st Person.	ಕೇಂಡ್ದುಪ್ಪ kēṇḍuḍuppa, we shall have heard.	ಕೇಂಡ್ದುಪ್ಪಯ kēṇḍuḍuppaya, we shall not have heard.
2nd „	ಕೇಂಡ್ದುಪ್ಪರ್ kēṇḍuḍupparu, you will have heard.	ಕೇಂಡ್ದುಪ್ಪಯರ್ kēṇḍuḍuppayaru, you will not have heard.
	&c. &c.	&c. &c.

IMPERATIVE MOOD.

Singular.

1st Person.	ಕೇಣುಗೆ kēṇuge, let me hear; I will hear.	ಕೇಣಂದೆ ಉಪ್ಪುಗೆ kēṇande uppuge, let me not hear.
2nd „	ಕೇಣ್ಲ kēṇla (ಕೇಣ್ kēṇu), hear, or do thou hear.	ಕೇಣಡ kēṇaḍa, ಕೇಣಂದೆ ಉಪ್ಪುಲ kēṇade uppula, do thou not hear.
	&c. &c.	&c. &c.

Plural.

1st Person.	ಕೇಣುಗ kēṇuga, let us hear.	ಕೇಣಂದೆ ಉಪ್ಪುಗ kēṇande uppuga, let us not hear.
2nd „	ಕೇಣ್ಲೆ kēṇule (ಕೇಣ್ಲೆ kēṇle), hear you, or do you hear.	ಕೇಣಂದೆ ಉಪ್ಪುಲೆ kēṇande uppule, ಕೇಣಡೆ kēṇaḍe, do you not hear.
	&c. &c.	&c. &c.

9

CONDITIONAL MOOD.

Singular.

	Positive.	*Negative.*
1st Person.	ಕೇಣ್ದ್ವೆ **kēṇuḍve,** I should hear.	ಕೇಣ್ದ್ವಯೆ **kēṇuḍvaye,** I should not hear.
2nd „	ಕೇಣ್ದ್ವ **kēṇuḍva,** thou wouldst hear.	ಕೇಣ್ದ್ವಯ **kēṇuḍvaya,** thou wouldst not hear.
	&c. &c.	&c. &c.

Plural.

1st Person.	ಕೇಣ್ದ್ವ **kēṇuḍva,** we should hear.	ಕೇಣ್ದ್ವಯ **kēṇuḍvaya,** we should not hear.
2nd „	ಕೇಣ್ದ್ವರ್ **kēṇuḍvaru,** you would hear.	ಕೇಣ್ದ್ವಯರ್ **kēṇuḍvayaru,** you would not hear.
	&c. &c.	&c. &c.

INFINITIVE MOOD.

PRESENT TENSE.

1st Infinitive.

ಕೇಣುನಿ **kēṇuni** (ಕೇಣುನೇ **kēṇunē**), (to) hear.	ಕೇಣಂದೆ ಉಪ್ಪುನಿ **kēṇande uppuni,** not (to) hear.

PAST TENSE.

IMPERFECT AND PERFECT.

ಕೇಂಡಿನಿ **kēṇḍini** (ಕೇಣ್ದಿನೇ **kēṇuḍinē**), (to) have heard. ಕೇಣ್ದಿನಿ **kēṇuḍini** (ಕೇಣ್ದಿನೇ **kēṇuḍinē**), (to) have had heard.	ಕೇಣಂದೆ ಇತ್ತಿನಿ **kēṇande ittini,** not (to) have heard.

2nd *Infinitive* (*Supine*).

	Positive.	*Negative.*
	ಕೇಣಿಯೆರೆ **kēṇiyere,** to hear.	ಕೇಣಂದೆ ಉಪ್ಪೆರೆ **kēṇande uppere,** not to hear.

GERUNDS AND PARTICIPLES.

PRESENT AND FUTURE.

Ger.	ಕೇಣೊಂಡು **kēṇoṇḍu,** hearing.	ಕೇಣಂದೆ **kēṇande,** not hearing.
Part.	ಕೇಣು **kēṇu,** hearing, that is hearing.	ಕೇಣಂದಿ **kēṇandi,** not hearing or that is not hearing.

PAST TENSE.

IMPERFECT.

Part.	ಕೇಂಡಿ **kēṇḍi,** that heard or that is heard.	ಕೇಣಂದಿ **kēṇandi,** not heard, that had or is not heard.

PERFECT.

Ger.	ಕೇಂಡ್ದ್ **kēṇḍuḍu,** having heard.	ಕೇಣಂದೆ **kēṇande,** having not heard.
Part.	ಕೇಂಡ್ದಿ **kēṇḍuḍi,** having heard or being heard, that has heard or that has been heard.	ಕೇಣಂದಿ **kēṇandi,** having or being not heard, that has not heard or that has not been heard.

PARTICIPIAL AND VERBAL NOUNS.

PRESENT AND FUTURE.

Singular.

Positive.	*Negative.*
Masc. ಕೇಣುನಾಯೆ **kēṇunāye,** he that hears.	ಕೇಣಂದಿನಾಯೆ **kēṇandināye,** he that does not hear.
Fem. ಕೇಣುನಾಳ್ **kēṇunāḷu,** she that hears.	ಕೇಣಂದಿನಾಳ್ **kēṇandināḷu,** she that does not hear.
Neut. ಕೇಣುನವು **kēṇunavu,** that which hears; or more frequently: the act of hearing.	ಕೇಣಂದಿನವು **kēṇandinavu,** that which does not hear.

Plural.

Masc. & fem. ಕೇಣುನಾಕುಳು **kēṇunākuḷu** / *Neut.* ಕೇಣುನೈಕುಳು **kēṇuneikuḷu** } those that hear.	ಕೇಣಂದಿನಾಕುಳು **kēṇandinākuḷu** / ಕೇಣಂದಿನೈಕುಳು **kēṇandineikuḷu** } those that do not hear.

PAST TENSE.

IMPERFECT.

Singular.

Masc. ಕೇಂಡಿನಾಯೆ **kēṇḍināye,** he that heard. &c. &c.	As in the present tense.

Plural.

Masc. & Fem. ಕೇಂಡಿನಾಕುಳು **kēṇḍinākuḷu,** they that heard. &c. &c.	Do.

PERFECT.

Singular.

Masc. ಕೇಂಡ್ದಿನಾಯೆ **kēṇḍuḍināye,** he that has heard.	Do
&c. &c.	

Plural.

Masc. & Fem. ಕೇಂಡ್ದಿನಾಕುಳು **kēṇḍuḍinākuḷu,** they that have heard.	Do.
&c. &c.	

SUBJUNCTIVE MOOD.

PRESENT TENSE.

Singular.

Positive.	*Negative.*
1st Person. ಕೇಣುವೆಡ **kēṇuveḍa,** if I hear.	ಕೇಣುಜೆಡ **kēṇujeḍa,** if I do not hear.
2nd „ ಕೇಣುವಡ **kēṇuvaḍa,** if thou hear (est.)	ಕೇಣುಜಡ **kēṇujaḍa,** if thou do (est) not hear.
&c. &c.	&c. &c.

Plural.

1st Person. ಕೇಣುವಡ **kēṇuvaḍa,** if we hear.	ಕೇಣುಜಡ **kēṇujaḍa,** if we do not hear.
2nd „ ಕೇಣುವರ್ಡ **kēṇuvaruḍa,** if you hear.	ಕೇಣುಜರ್ಡ **kēṇujaruḍa,** if you do not hear.
&c. &c.	&c. &c.

PAST TENSE.

Singular.

	Positive.	*Negative.*
1st Person.	ಕೇಂಡೆಡ **kēṇḍeḍa,** if I heard.	ಕೇಂಡಿಜಿಡ **kēṇḍijiḍa,** if I did not hear.
2nd „	ಕೇಂಡಡ **kēṇḍaḍa,** if thou heard (st.)	ಕೇಂಡಿಜಡ **kēṇḍijaḍa,** if thou did (st) not hear.
	&c. &c.	&c. &c.

Plural.

1st Person.	ಕೇಂಡಡ **kēṇḍaḍa,** if we heard.	ಕೇಂಡಿಜಡ **kēṇḍijaḍa,** if we did not hear.
2nd „	ಕೇಂಡರ್ಡ **kēṇḍaruḍa,** if you heard.	ಕೇಂಡಿಜರ್ಡ **kēṇḍijaruḍa,** if you did not hear.
	&c. &c.	&c. &c.

POTENTIAL MOOD.

ಕೇಣೊಲಿ **kēṇoli** (ಕೇಣ್ **kēṇu**+ಒಲಿ **oli**), I &c. may hear.	ಕೇಣಿಯೆರೆ ಬಲ್ಲಿ **kēṇiyere balli,** I &c. may not hear.
ಕೇಣೊಡು **kēṇoḍu** (ಕೇಣ್ **kēṇu**+ಬೋಡು, **bōḍu**) I &c. must or need hear.	ಕೇಣೊಡ್ಡಿ **kēṇoḍḍi,** I &c. must not or need not hear.
ಕೇಣಿಯೆರೆ **kēṇiyere** { ತೀರುಂಡು **tīrunḍu** / ತೆರಿಯುಂಡು **teriyunḍu** / ಕೂಡುಂಡು **kūḍunḍu** } I &c. can hear or know (how) to hear.	ಕೇಣಿಯೆರೆ **kēṇiyere** { ತೀರುಜಿ **tīruji** / ತೆರಿಯುಜಿ **teriyuji** / ಕೂಡುಜಿ **kūḍuji** } I &c. cannot hear or know not (how) to hear.

CONTINUED FORM.

ಕೇಣೊಂಡು ಉಪ್ಪುನಿ **kēṇoṇḍu uppuni**, to be hearing.

Singular.

	Positive.	*Negative.*
1st Person.	ಕೇಣೊಂಡು ಉಪ್ಪುವೆ **kēṇoṇḍu uppuve,** I am hearing.	ಕೇಣೊಂಡು ಉಪ್ಪುಜಿ **kēṇoṇḍu uppuji,** I am not hearing.
	&c. &c.	&c. &c.

Plural.

1st Person.	ಕೇಣೊಂಡು ಉಪ್ಪುವ **kēṇoṇḍu uppuva,** we are hearing.	ಕೇಣೊಂಡು ಉಪ್ಪುಜ **kēṇoṇḍu uppuja,** we are not hearing.
	&c &c.	&c &c.

FREQUENTATIVE FORM.

PRESENT AND FUTURE TENSES.

	Singular.	*Plural.*
1st Person.	ಕೇಣೇವೆ **kēṇēve** I hear again and again.	ಕೇಣೇವ **kēṇēva,** we hear again and again.
	&c. &c.	&c. &c.

PAST TENSE.

	Singular.	*Plural.*
1st Person.	**ಕೇಣೇದೆ kēṇēde,** I heard again and again.	**ಕೇಣೇದ kēṇēda,** we heard again and again.
	&c. &c.	&c. &c.

INTENSIVE FORM.

	Present tense.	*Past tense.*
1st Person.	**ಕೇಂಡ್ರುವೆ kēṇḍruve,** I hear energetically.	**ಕೇಂಡ್ರಿಯೆ kēṇḍriye,** I heard energetically.
	&c. &c.	&c. &c.

91. 3rd Conjugation of Verbs ending in ರು **ru.**

Crude form: ಬೂರು **būru,** to fall.

INDICATIVE MOOD.

PRESENT TENSE.

Singular.

	Positive.	*Negative.*
1st Person.	**ಬೂರುವೆ būruve,** I fall.	**ಬೂರುಜಿ būruji,** I do not fall.
2nd „	**ಬೂರುವ būruva,** thou fallest.	**ಬೂರುಜ būruja,** thou doest not fall.
	&c. &c.	&c. &c.

Plural.

	Positive.	*Negative.*
1st Person.	ಬೂರುವ būruva, we fall.	ಬೂರುಜ būruja, we do not fall.
2nd „	ಬೂರುವರ್ būruvarụ, you fall.	ಬೂರುಜರ್ būrujarụ, you do not fall.
	&c. &c.	&c. &c.

PAST TENSE.

IMPERFECT.

Singular.

1st Person.	ಬೂರಿಯೆ būriye, I fell.	ಬೂರಿಜಿ būriji, I did not fall.
2nd „	ಬೂರಿಯ būriya, thou fellest.	ಬೂರಿಜ būrija, thou didst not fall.
	&c. &c.	&c. &c.

Plural.

1st Person.	ಬೂರಿಯ būriya, we fell.	ಬೂರಿಜ būrija, we did not fall.
2nd „	ಬೂರಿಯರ್ būriyarụ, you fell.	ಬೂರಿಜರ್ burijarụ, you did not fall.
	&c. &c.	&c. &c.

PERFECT.

Singular.

	Positive.	*Negative.*
1st Person.	ಬೂರುದೆ **būrude**, I have fallen.	ಬೂರುದಿಜಿ **būrudiji**, I have not fallen.
2nd „	ಬೂರುದ **būruda**, thou hast fallen.	ಬೂರುದಿಜ **būrudija**, thou hast not fallen.
	&c. &c.	&c. &c.

Plural.

1st Person.	ಬೂರುದ **būruda**, we have fallen.	ಬೂರುದಿಜ **būrudija**, we have not fallen.
2nd „	ಬೂರುದರ್ **būrudaru̥**, you have fallen.	ಬೂರುದಿಜರ್ **būrudijaru̥**, you have not fallen.
	&c. &c.	&c. &c.

PLUPERFECT TENSE.

Singular.

1st Person.	ಬೂರುದಿತ್ತೆ **būruditte** (ಬೂರುದು+ಇತ್ತೆ **būrudu itte**), I had fallen.	ಬೂರುದಿತ್ತ್ುಜಿ **būrudittu̥ji**, I had not fallen.
2nd „	ಬೂರುದಿತ್ತ **būruditta**, thou hadst fallen.	ಬೂರುದಿತ್ತ್ುಜ **būrudittu̥ja**, thou hadst not fallen.
	&c. &c.	&c. &c.

Plural.

	Positive.	*Negative.*
1st Person.	ಬೂರುದಿತ್ತ **būruditta,** we had fallen.	ಬೂರುದಿತ್ತ್‌ಜ **būrudittụja,** we had not fallen.
2nd „	ಬೂರುದಿತ್ತರ್ **būrudittarụ,** you had fallen.	ಬೂರುದಿತ್ತ್‌ಜರ್ **būrudittụjarụ,** you had not fallen.
	&c. &c.	&c. &c.

FUTURE TENSE.

1st FUTURE.

Singular.

1st Person.	ಬೂರೆ **būre,** I shall fall.	ಬೂರಯೆ **būraye,** I shall not fall.
2nd „	ಬೂರ **būra,** thou wilt fall.	ಬೂರಯ **būraya,** thou wilt not fall.
	&c. &c.	&c. &c.

Plural.

1st Person.	ಬೂರ **būra,** we shall fall.	ಬೂರಯ **būraya,** we shall not fall.
2nd „	ಬೂರರ್ **būrarụ,** you will fall.	ಬೂರಯರ್ **būrayarụ,** you will not fall.
	&c. &c.	&c. &c.

2nd FUTURE (FUTURE PERFECT).

(ಬೂರುದು **būrudu**, *Gerund Perfect* and ಉಪ್ಪೆ **uppe**, etc. *Future Tense* of ಉಪ್ಪುನಿ **uppuni.**)

Singular.

	Positive.	*Negative.*
1st Person.	ಬೂರುದುಪ್ಪೆ **būruduppe,** I shall have fallen.	ಬೂರುದುಪ್ಪಯೆ **būruduppaye,** I shall not have fallen.
2nd „	ಬೂರುದುಪ್ಪ **būruduppa,** thou wilt have fallen.	ಬೂರುದುಪ್ಪಯ **būruduppaya,** thou wilt not have fallen.
	&c. &c.	&c. &c.

Plural.

1st Person.	ಬೂರುದುಪ್ಪ **būruduppa,** we shall have fallen.	ಬೂರುದುಪ್ಪಯ **buruduppaya,** we shall not have fallen.
2nd „	ಬೂರುದುಪ್ಪರ್ **būrudupparu̥,** you will have fallen.	ಬೂರುದುಪ್ಪಯರ್ **būruduppayaru̥,** you will not have fallen.
	&c. &c.	&c. &c.

IMPERATIVE MOOD.

Singular.

1st Person.	ಬೂರುಗೆ **būruge,** let me fall; I will fall.	ಬೂರಂದೆ ಉಪ್ಪುಗೆ **būrande uppuge,** let me not fall; I will not fall.
2nd „	ಬೂರ್ಲ **būrla** (ಬೂರು **būru**), fall, or do thou fall.	ಬೂರಡ **būraḍa,** ಬೂರಂದೆ ಉಪ್ಪುಲ **būrande uppula,** do thou not fall.
	&c. &c.	&c. &c.

Plural.

	Positive.	*Negative.*
1st Person.	ಬೂರುಗ **būruga,** let us fall.	ಬೂರಂದೆ ಉಪ್ಪುಗ **būrande uppuga,** let us not fall.
2nd „	ಬೂರುಲೆ **būrule,** fall you, or do you fall.	ಬೂರಡೆ **būraḍe,** ಬೂರಂದೆ ಉಪ್ಪುಲೆ **būrande uppule,** do you not fall.
	&c. &c.	&c. &c.

CONDITIONAL MOOD.

Singular.

1st Person.	ಬೂರುದ್ವೆ **būrudve,** I should fall.	ಬೂರುದ್ವಯೆ **būrudvaye,** I should not fall.
2nd „	ಬೂರುದ್ವ **būrudva,** thou wouldst fall.	ಬೂರುದ್ವಯಃ **būrudvaya,** thou wouldst not fall.
	&c. &c.	&c. &c.

Plural.

1st Person.	ಬೂರುದ್ವ **būrudva,** we should fall.	ಬೂರುದ್ವಯ **būrudvaya,** we should not fall.
2nd „	ಬೂರುದ್ವರ್ **būrudvaru̥,** you would fall.	ಬೂರುದ್ವಯರ್ **būrudvayaru̥,** you would not fall.
	&c. &c.	&c. &c.

Positive.	*Negative.*
ಬೂರುನಿ **būruni** (ಬೂರುನೇ **būrunē**), (to) fall.	ಬೂರಂದೆ ಉಪ್ಪುನಿ **būrande uppuni,** not (to) fall.

PAST TENSE.

IMPERFECT AND PERFECT.

ಬೂರಿನಿ **būrini** (ಬೂರಿನೇ **būrinē**), (to) have fallen. ಬೂರುದಿನಿ **būrudini** (ಬೂರುದಿನೇ **būrudinē**), (to) have had fallen.	ಬೂರಂದೆ ಇತ್ತಿನಿ **būrande ittini,** not (to) have fallen.

2nd *Infinitive* (*Supine*).

ಬೂರಿಯೆರೆ **būriyere** (ಬೂರೆರೆ **būrere**), to fall.	ಬೂರಂದೆ ಉಪ್ಪೆರೆ **būrande uppere,** not to fall.

GERUNDS AND PARTICIPLES.

PRESENT AND FUTURE.

Ger. ಬೂರೊಣ್ಡು **būroṇḍu,** falling.	ಬೂರಂದೆ **būrande,** not falling.
Part. ಬೂರು **būru,** falling or that is falling.	ಬೂರಂದಿ **būrandi,** not falling or that is not falling.

PAST TENSE.

IMPERFECT.

Positive.	*Negative.*
Part. ಬೂರಿ būri, fallen, that fell or that has fallen.	ಬೂರಂದಿ būrandi, not fallen, that has or had not fallen.

PERFECT.

Ger. ಬೂರುದು būrudu, having fallen.	ಬೂರಂದೆ būrande, having not fallen.
Part. ಬೂರುದಿ būrudi, having fallen or that has fallen.	ಬೂರಂದಿ būrandi, having not fallen, or that has not fallen.

PARTICIPIAL AND VERBAL NOUNS.

PRESENT AND FUTURE.

Singular.

Mas. ಬೂರುನಾಯೆ būrunāye, he that falls.	ಬೂರಂದಿನಾಯೆ būrandināye, he that does not fall.
Fem. ಬೂರುನಾಳ್ būrunāḷụ, she that falls.	ಬೂರಂದಿನಾಳ್ būrandināḷụ, she that does not fall.
Neut. ಬೂರುನವು būrunavu, that which falls; or more frequently: the act of falling.	ಬೂರಂದಿನವು būrandinavu, that which does not fall.

Plural.

	Positive.		*Negative*	
Masc. & Fem.	ಬೂರುನಾಕುಳು būrunākuḷu	thouse that fall.	ಬೂರಂದಿನಾಕುಳು būrandinākuḷu	those that do not fall.
Neut.	ಬೂರುನೈಕುಳು būruneikuḷu		ಬೂರಂದಿನೈಕುಳು būrandineikuḷu	

PAST TENSE.

IMPERFECT.

Singular.

Masc.	ಬೂರಿನಾಯೆ būrināye, he that fell. &c. &c.	As in the present tense.

Plural.

Masc. & Fem.	ಬೂರಿನಾಕುಳು būrinākuḷu, they that fell. &c. &c.	Do.

PERFECT.

Singular.

Masc.	ಬೂರುದಿನಾಯೆ būrudināye, he that has fallen. &c. &c.	Do.

Plural.

Positive.	*Negative.*
Masc. & Fem. ಬೂರುದಿನಾಕುಳು **būrudinākuḷu,** those that have fallen.	ಬೂರಂದಿನಾಕುಳು **būrandinākuḷu,** those that have not fallen.
&c.	&c.

CONDITIONAL FORM.

PRESENT TENSE.

Singular.

1st Person.	ಬೂರುವೆಡ **būruveḍa,** if I fall.	ಬೂರುಜೆಡ **būrujeḍa,** if I do not fall.
2nd „	ಬೂರುವಡ **būruvaḍa,** if thou fall(est.)	ಬೂರುಜಡ **būrujaḍa,** if thou do(est) not fall.
	&c. &c.	&c. &c.

Plural.

1st Person.	ಬೂರುವಡ **būruvaḍa,** if we fall.	ಬೂರುಜಡ **būrujaḍa,** if we do not fall.
2nd „	ಬೂರುವರ್ಡ **būruvaruḍa,** if you fall.	ಬೂರುಜರ್ಡ **būrujaruḍa,** if you do not fall.
	&c. &c.	&c. &c.

PAST TENSE.

Singular.

	Positive.	*Negative.*
1st Person.	ಬೂರಿಯೆಡ **būriyeḍa**, if I fell.	ಬೂರಿಜೆಡ **būrijeḍa**, if I did not fall.
2nd „	ಬೂರಿಯಡ **būriyaḍa**, if thou fell(est), or if thou didst fall.	ಬೂರಿಜಡ **būrijaḍa**, if thou did(st) not fall.
	&c. &c.	&c. &c.

Plural.

	Positive.	*Negative.*
1st Person.	ಬೂರಿಯಡ **būriyaḍa**, if we fell.	ಬೂರಿಜಡ **būrijaḍa**, if we did not fall.
2nd „	ಬೂರಿಯರ್ಡ **būriyaruḍa**, if you fell.	ಬೂರಿಜರ್ಡ **būrijaruḍa**, if you did not fall.
	&c. &c.	&c. &c.

POTENTIAL MOOD.

Positive	Negative
ಬೂರೊಲಿ **būroli** (ಬೂರು **būru**+ ಒಲಿ **oli**), I &c. may fall.	ಬೂರಿಯೆರೆ ಬಲ್ಲಿ **būriyere balli**, I &c. may not fall.
ಬೂರೊಡು **būroḍu** (ಬೂರು **būru**+ಬೋಡು **bōḍu**), I &c. must or need fall.	ಬೂರೊಡ್ಚಿ **būroḍči**, I &c. must not or need not fall.
ಬೂರಿಯೆರೆ **būriyere** { ತೀರುಂಡು **tīrunḍu** / ತೆರಿಯುಂಡು **teriyunḍu** / ಕೂಡುಂಡು **kūḍunḍu** } I &c. can fall or know (how) to fall.	ಬೂರಿಯೆರೆ { ತೀರುಜಿ **tīruji** / ತೆರಿಯುಜಿ **teriyuji** / ಕೂಡುಜಿ **kūḍuji** } I &c. cannot fall or know not (how) to fall.

CONTINUED FORM.

ಬೂರೊಣ್ಡು ಉಪ್ಪುನಿ **būroṇḍu uppui**, to be falling.

Singular.

Positive.	*Negative.*
1st Person. ಬೂರೊಣ್ಡು ಉಪ್ಪುವೆ **būroṇḍu uppuve**, I am falling.	ಬೂರೊಣ್ಡು ಉಪ್ಪುಜಿ **būroṇḍu uppuji**, I am not falling.
&c. &c.	&c. &c.

Plural.

1st Person. ಬೂರೊಣ್ಡು ಉಪ್ಪುವ **būroṇḍu uppuva**, we are falling.	ಬೂರೊಣ್ಡು ಉಪ್ಪುಜ **būroṇḍu uppuja**, we are not falling.
&c &c.	&c. &c.

FREQUENTATIVE.

PRESENT AND FUTURE TENSES.

Singular.	*Plural.*
1st Person. ಬೂರೇವೆ **būrēve**, I fall again and again.	ಬೂರೇವ **būrēva**, we fall again and again.
&c. &c.	&c. &c.

PAST TENSE.

	Singular.	*Plural.*
1st Person.	ಬೂರೇದೆ **būrēde**, I fell again and again.	ಬೂರೇದ **būrēda**, we fell again and again.
	&c. &c.	&c. &c.

INTENSIVE FORM.

	Present tense.	*Past tense.*
1st Person	ಬೂರ್ಡುವೆ **būrḍuve**, I fall energetically.	ಬೂರ್ಡಿಯೆ **būrḍiye**, I fell energetically.
	&c. &c.	&c. &c.

92. 4th Conjugation of Verbs ending in ಪಿ pi.

Crude form: ತೂಪಿ tūpi, to see.

INDICATIVE MOOD.

PRESENT TENSE.

Singular.

	Positive.	*Negative.*
1st Person.	ತೂಪೆ **tūpe**, I see.	ತೂಪುಜಿ **tūpuji**, I do not see.
2nd „	ತೂಪ **tūpa**, thou seest.	ತೂಪುಜ **tūpuja**, thou doest not see.
3rd *Masc.*	ತೂಪೆ **tūpe**, he sees.	ತೂಪುಜೆ **tūpuje**, he does not see.
„ „ *Fem.*	ತೂಪಳ್ **tūpaḷu**, she sees.	ತೂಪುಜಳ್ **tūpujaḷu**, she does not see.
„ „ *Neut.*	ತೂಪುಂಡು **tūpuṇḍu**, it sees.	ತೂಪುಜಿ **tūpuji**, it does not see.

Plural.

		Positive.	Negative.
1st Person.		ತೂಪ tūpa, we see.	ತೂಪುಜ tūpuja, we do not see.
2nd „		ತೂಪರ್ tūparu̥, you see.	ತೂಪುಜರ್ tūpujaru̥, you do not see.
3rd „	*Mas.*	ತೂಪೆರ್ tūperu̥ } they see.	ತೂಪುಜೆರ್ tūpujeru̥ } they do not see.
„ „	*Fem.*	ತೂಪೆರ್ tūperu̥ } they see.	ತೂಪುಜೆರ್ tūpujeru̥ } they do not see.
„ „	*Neut.*	ತೂಪ tūpa } they see.	ತೂಪುಜ tūpuja } they do not see.

PAST TENSE.

IMPERFECT.

Singular.

1st Person.		ತೂಯೆ tūye, I saw.	ತೂಯಿಜಿ tūyiji, I did not see.
2nd „		ತೂಯ tūya, thou sawest.	ತೂಯಿಜ tūyija, thou didst not see.
3rd „	*Masc.*	ತೂಯೆ tūye, he saw.	ತೂಯಿಜೆ tūyije, he did not see.
„ „	*Fem.*	ತೂಯಳ್ tūyaḷu̥, she saw.	ತೂಯಿಜಳ್ tūyijaḷu̥, she did not see.
„ „	*Neut.*	ತೂಂಡು tūṇḍu, it saw.	ತೂಯಿಜಿ tūyiji, it did not see.

Plural.

	Positive.		*Negative.*	
1st Person.	ತೂಯ **tūya,** we saw.		ತೂಯಿಜ **tūyija,** we did not see.	
2nd „	ತೂಯರ್ **tūyaru̥,** you saw.		ತೂಯಿಜರ್ **tūyijaru̥,** you did not see.	
3rd „ *Masc.*	ತೂಯೆರ್ **tūyeru̥**	they saw.	ತೂಯಿಜೆರ್ **tūyijeru̥**	they did not see.
„ „ *Fem.*	ತೂಯೆರ್ **tūyeru̥**	they saw.	ತೂಯಿಜೆರ್ **tūyijeru̥**	they did not see.
„ „ *Neut.*	ತೂಯ **tūya**	they saw.	ತೂಯಿಜ **tūyija**	they did not see.

PERFECT.

Singular.

1st Person.	ತೂತೆ **tūte,** I have seen.	ತೂತಿಜಿ **tūtiji,** I have not seen.
2nd „	ತೂತ **tūta,** thou hast seen.	ತೂತಿಜ **tūtija,** thou hast not seen.
3rd „ *Masc.*	ತೂತೆ **tūte,** he has seen.	ತೂತಿಜೆ **tūtije,** he has not seen.
„ „ *Fem.*	ತೂತಳ್ **tūtaḷu̥,** she has seen.	ತೂತಿಜಳ್ **tūtijaḷu̥,** she has not seen.
„ „ *Neut.*	ತೂತ್ಂಡ್ **tūtu̥ṇḍu̥,** it has seen.	ತೂತಿಜಿ **tūtiji,** it has not seen.

Plural.

	Positive.		Negative.	
1st Person.	ತೂತ **tūta**, we have seen.		ತೂತಿಜ **tūtija**, we have not seen.	
2nd „	ತೂತರ್ **tūtarụ**, you have seen.		ತೂತಿಜರ್ **tūtijarụ**, you have not seen.	
3rd „ *Masc.*	ತೂತೆರ್ **tūterụ**	they have seen.	ತೂತಿಜೆರ್ **tūtijerụ**	they have not seen.
„ „ *Fem.*	ತೂತೆರ್ **tūterụ**	they have seen.	ತೂತಿಜೆರ್ **tūtijerụ**	they have not seen.
„ „ *Neut.*	ತೂತ **tūta**	they have seen.	ತೂತಿಜ **tutija**	they have not seen.

PLUPERFECT TENSE.

Singular.

	Positive	Negative
1st Person.	ತೂದಿತ್ತೆ **tūditte**, I had seen.	ತೂದಿತ್ತಿಜಿ **tūdittiji**, I had not seen.
2nd „	ತೂದಿತ್ತ **tūditta**, thou hadst seen.	ತೂದಿತ್ತಿಜ **tūdittija**, thou hadst not seen.
3rd „ *Masc.*	ತೂದಿತ್ತೆ **tūditte**, he had seen.	ತೂದಿತ್ತಿಜೆ **tūdittije**, he had not seen.
„ „ *Fem.*	ತೂದಿತ್ತಳ್ **tūdittaḷụ**, she had seen.	ತೂದಿತ್ತಿಜಳ್ **tūdittijaḷụ**, she had not seen.
„ „ *Neut.*	ತೂದಿತ್ತುಂಡ್ **tūdittuṇḍụ**, it had seen.	ತೂದಿತ್ತಿಜಿ **tūdittiji**, it had not seen.

Plural.

		Positive.	*Negative.*
1st Person.		ತೂದಿತ್ತ **tūditta,** we had seen.	ತೂದಿತ್ತಿಜ **tūdittija,** we had not seen.
2nd „		ತೂದಿತ್ತರ್ **tūdittarụ,** you had seen.	ತೂದಿತ್ತಿಜರ್ **tūdittijarụ,** you had not seen.
3rd „	*Masc.*	ತೂದಿತ್ತೆರ್ **tūditterụ** } they had seen.	ತೂದಿತ್ತಿಜೆರ್ **tūdittijerụ** } they had not seen.
„ „	*Fem.*	ತೂದಿತ್ತೆರ್ **tūditterụ** } they had seen.	ತೂದಿತ್ತಿಜೆರ್ **tūdittijerụ** } they had not seen.
„ „	*Neut.*	ತೂದಿತ್ತ **tūditta** } they had seen.	ತೂದಿತ್ತಿಜ **tūdittija** } they had not seen.

FUTURE TENSE.

1st FUTURE.

Singular.

1st Person.		ತೂವೆ **tūve,** I shall see.	ತೂವಯೆ **tūvaye,** I shall not see.
2nd „		ತೂವ **tūva,** thou wilt see.	ತೂವಯ **tūvaya,** thou wilt not see.
3rd „	*Masc.*	ತೂವೆ **tūve,** he will see.	ತೂವಯೆ **tūvaye,** he will not see.
„ „	*Fem.*	ತೂವಳ್ **tūvaḷụ,** she will see.	ತೂವಯಳ್ **tūvayaḷụ,** she will not see.
„ „	*Neut.*	ತೂವು **tūvu,** it will see.	ತೂವಂದ್ **tūvandụ,** it will not see.

Plural.

	Positive.	*Negative*
1st Person.	ತೂವ tūva, we shall see.	ತೂವಯ tūvaya, we shall not see.
2nd "	ತೂವರ್ tūvaru̥, you will see.	ತೂವಯರ್ tūvayaru̥, you will not see.
3rd " *Masc.*	ತೂವೆರ್ tūveru̥ } they will see.	ತೂವಯೆರ್ tūvayeru̥ } they will not see.
" " *Fem.*	ತೂವೆರ್ tūveru̥ } they will see.	ತೂವಯೆರ್ tūvayeru̥ } they will not see.
" " *Neut.*	ತೂವ tūva } they will see.	ತೂವಯ tūvaya } they will not see.

2nd FUTURE (FUTURE PERFECT).

(ತೂದು tūdu, *Gerund Perfect* and ಉಪ್ಪೆ uppe, etc. *Future tense* of ಉಪ್ಪುನಿ uppuni, to be.)

Singular.

1st Person.	ತೂದುಪ್ಪೆ tūduppe, I shall have seen.	ತೂದುಪ್ಪಯೆ tūduppaye, I shall not have seen.
2nd "	ತೂದುಪ್ಪ tūduppa, thou wilt have seen.	ತೂದುಪ್ಪಯ tūduppaya, thou wilt not have seen.
3rd " *Masc.*	ತೂದುಪ್ಪೆ tūduppe, he will have seen.	ತೂದುಪ್ಪಯೆ tūduppaye, he will not have seen.
12 " " *Fem.*	ತೂದುಪ್ಪಳ್ tūduppaḷu̥, she will have seen.	ತೂದುಪ್ಪಯಳ್ tūduppayaḷu̥, she will not have seen.
" " *Neut.*	ತೂದುಪ್ಪು tūduppu, it will have seen.	ತೂದುಪ್ಪಂದ್ tūduppandu̥, it will not have seen.

Plural.

	Positive.	*Negative.*
1st Person.	ತೂದುಪ್ಪ **tūduppa,** we shall have seen.	ತೂದುಪ್ಪಯ **tūduppya,** we shall not have seen.
2nd „	ತೂದುಪ್ಪರ್ **tūdupparu̥,** you will have seen.	ತೂದುಪ್ಪಯರ್ **tūduppayaru̥,** you will not have seen.
3rd „ *Masc.*	ತೂದುಪ್ಪೆರ್ **tūdupperu̥** } they will have seen.	ತೂದುಪ್ಪಯೆರ್ **tūduppayeru̥** } they will not have seen.
„ „ *Fem.*	ತೂದುಪ್ಪೆರ್ **tūdupperu̥** } they will have seen.	ತೂದುಪ್ಪಯೆರ್ **tūduppayeru̥** } they will not have seen.
„ „ *Neut.*	ತೂದುಪ್ಪ **tūduppa** } they will have seen.	ತೂದುಪ್ಪಯ **tūduppaya** } they will not have seen.

IMPERATIVE MOOD.

Singular.

1st Person.	ತೂಕೆ **tūke,** let me see; I will see.	ತೂವಂದೆ ಉಪ್ಪುಗೆ **tūvande uppuge,** let me not see.
2nd „	ತೂಲ **tūla,** see, or do thou see.	ತೂವಡ **tūvaḍa,** do thou not see.
3rd „	ತೂವಡ್ **tūvaḍu̥,** let him, her, or it see.	ತೂವಂದೆ ಉಪ್ಪಡ್ **tūvande uppaḍu̥,** let him, her or it not see.

Plural.

1st Person.	ತೂಕ **tūka,** let us see.	ತೂವಂದೆ ಉಪ್ಪುಗ **tūvande uppuga,** let us not see.
2nd „	ತೂಲೆ **tūle,** see you or do you see.	ತೂವಡೆ **tūvaḍe,** do you not see.
3rd „	ತೂವಡ್ **tūvaḍu̥,** let them see.	ತೂವಂದೆ ಉಪ್ಪಡ್ **tūvande uppaḍu̥,** let them not see.

CONDITIONAL MOOD.

Singular.

	Positive.	*Negative.*
1st Person.	ತೂತ್ವೆ **tūtve**, I should see.	ತೂತ್ವಯೆ **tūtvaye**, I should not see.
2nd „	ತೂತ್ವ **tūtva**, thou wouldst see.	ತೂತ್ವಯ **tūtvaya**, thou wouldst not see.
3rd „ *Masc.*	ತೂತ್ವೆ **tūtve**, he would see.	ತೂತ್ವಯೆ **tūtvaye**, he would not see.
„ „ *Fem.*	ತೂತ್ವಳ್ **tūtvaḷụ**, she would see.	ತೂತ್ವಯಳ್ **tūtvayaḷụ**, she would not see.
„ „ *Neut.*	ತೂತು **tūtu**, it would see.	ತೂತ್ವಂದ್ **tūtvandụ**, it would not see.

Plural.

1st Person.	ತೂತ್ವ **tūtva**, we should see.	ತೂತ್ವಯ **tūtvaya**, we should not see.
2nd „	ತೂತ್ವರ್ **tūtvarụ**, you would see.	ತೂತ್ವಯರ್ **tūtvayarụ**, you would not see.
3rd „ *Masc.*	ತೂತ್ವೆರ್ **tūtverụ** } they would see.	ತೂತ್ವಯೆರ್ **tūtvayerụ** } they would not see.
„ „ *Fem.*	ತೂತ್ವೆರ್ **tūtverụ** } they would see.	ತೂತ್ವಯೆರ್ **tūtvayerụ** } they would not see.
„ „ *Neut.*	ತೂತ್ವ **tūtva** } they would see.	ತೂತ್ವಯ **tūtvaya** } they would not see.

INFINITIVE MOOD.

PRESENT TENSE.

1*st Infinitive.*

ತೂಪಿನಿ **tūpini** (ತೂಪಿನೇ **tūpinē**), (to) see. | ತೂವಂದೆ ಉಪ್ಪುನಿ **tūvande uppuni**, not (to) see.

PAST TENSE.

IMPERFECT AND PERFECT.

Positive.	*Negative.*
ತೂಯಿನಿ tūyini (ತೂಯಿನೇ tūyinē), (to) have seen. ತೂತಿನಿ tūtini (ತೂತಿನೇ tūtinē), (to) have had seen.	ತೂವಂದೆ ಇತ್ತಿನಿ tūvande ittini, not (to) have seen.

2nd Infinitive (Supine).

ತೂವೆರೆ tūvere, to see.	ತೂವಂದೆ ಉಪ್ಪೆರೆ tūvande uppere, not to see.

GERUNDS AND PARTICIPLES.

PRESENT AND FUTURE.

Ger. ತೂವೊಣ್ಡು tūvoṇḍu, seeing.	ತೂವಂದೆ tūvande, not seeing.
Part. ತೂಪಿ tūpi, seeing, that is seeing.	ತೂವಂದಿ tūvandi, not seeing or that is not seeing.

PAST TENSE.

IMPERFECT.

Part. ತೂಯಿ tūyi, that saw, or that is seen.	ತೂವಂದಿ tūvandi, not seen, that had or is not seen.

PERFECT.

	Positive.	Negative.
Ger.	ತೂದು tūdu, having seen.	ತೂವಂದೆ tūvande, having not seen.
Part.	ತೂತಿ tūti, having or being seen, that has, or has been, seen.	ತೂವಂದಿ tūvandi, having or being not seen, that has not, or has not been, seen.

PARTICIPIAL AND VERBAL NOUNS.

Masc.	ತೂಪಿನಾಯೆ tūpināye, he that sees.	ತೂವಂದಿನಾಯೆ tūvandināye, he that does not see.
	&c. &c.	&c. &c.

SUBJUNCTIVE MOOD.

PRESENT TENSE.

Singular.

1st Person.	ತೂಪೆಡ tūpeḍa, if I see.	ತೂಪುಜೆಡ tūpujeḍa, If I do not see.
2nd „	ತೂಪಡ tūpaḍa, if thou see(st).	ತೂಪುಜಡ tūpujaḍa, if thou do(est) not see.
	&c. &c.	&c. &c.

POTENTIAL MOOD.

ತೂವೊಲಿ tūvoli (ತೂ tū+ಒಲಿ oli), I &c. may see.	ತೂವೆರೆ ಬಲ್ಲಿ tūvere balli, I &c. may not see.
ತೂವೊಡು tūvoḍu (ತೂ tū+ಬೋಡು bōḍu), I &c. must or need see.	ತೂವೊಡ್ಚಿ tūvoḍči, (ತೂಪಿ tūpi+ಬೋಡು bōḍu+ಇಜ್ಜಿ ijji), I &c. must not or need not see.
&c. &c.	&c. &c.

The rest are regular.

CONTINUED FORM.

	Positive.	*Negative.*
Masc.	ತೂವೊಣ್ದು ಉಪ್ಪುವೆ **tūvoṇḍu uppuve,** I am seeing.	ತೂವೊಣ್ದು ಉಪ್ಪುಜಿ **tūvoṇḍu uppuji,** I am not seeing.
	&c. &c.	&c. &c.

Frequentative **&c. regular.**

93. 5th Conjugation of Verbs ending in ಪಿ pi.

Crude form: ಪಣ್ಪಿ **paṇpi,** to say.

INDICATIVE MOOD.

PRESENT TENSE.

Singular.

1st Person.	ಪಣ್ಪೆ **paṇpe,** I say.	ಪಣ್ಪುಜಿ **paṇpuji,** I do not say.
2nd „	ಪಣ್ಪ **paṇpa,** thou sayest.	ಪಣ್ಪುಜ **paṇpuja,** thou doest not say.
3rd „ *Masc.*	ಪಣ್ಪೆ **paṇpe,** he says.	ಪಣ್ಪುಜೆ **paṇpuje,** he does not say.
	&c. &c.	&c. &c.

Plural.

1st Person.	ಪಣ್ಪ **paṇpa,** we say.	ಪಣ್ಪುಜ **paṇpuja,** we do not say.
2nd „	ಪಣ್ಪರ್ **paṇparu̥,** you say.	ಪಣ್ಪುಜರ್ **paṇpujaru̥,** you do not say.
	&c. &c.	&c. &c.

PAST TENSE.

IMPERFECT.

Singular.

	Positive.	*Negative.*
1st Person.	ಪಂಡೆ paṇḍe, I said.	ಪಂಡಿಜಿ paṇḍiji, I did not say.
2nd „	ಪಂಡ paṇḍa, thou saidst.	ಪಂಡಿಜ paṇḍija, thou didst not say.
	&c. &c.	&c. &c.

Plural.

1st Person.	ಪಂಡ paṇḍa, we said.	ಪಂಡಿಜ paṇḍija, we did not say.
2nd „	ಪಂಡರ್ paṇḍarụ, you said.	ಪಂಡಿಜರ್ paṇḍijarụ, you did not say.
	&c. &c.	&c. &c.

PERFECT.

Singular.

1st Person.	ಪಣ್ತೆ paṇte, I have said.	ಪಣ್ತಿಜಿ paṇtiji, I have not said.
2nd „	ಪಣ್ತ paṇta, thou hast said.	ಪಣ್ತಿಜ paṇtija, thou hast not said.
	&c. &c.	&c. &c.

Pluperfect liko tho preceding conjugation.

FUTURE TENSE.

1st FUTURE.

Singular.

	Positive.	*Negative.*
1st Person.	ಪಣ್ಂಬೆ paṇụmbe, I shall say.	ಪಣಯೆ paṇaye, I shall not say.
2nd „	ಪಣ್ಂಬ paṇụmba, thou wilt say.	ಪಣಯ paṇaya, thou wilt not say.
	&c. &c.	&c. &c.

Plural.

1st Person.	ಪಣ್ಂಬ paṇụmba, we shall say.	ಪಣಯ paṇaya, we shall not say.
2nd „	ಪಣ್ಂಬರ್ paṇụmbarụ, you will say.	ಪಣಯರ್ paṇayarụ, you will not say.
	&c. &c.	&c. &c.

2nd FUTURE (FUTURE PERFECT).

(ಪಂಡ್ದ್ paṇḍụdụ, *Past Gerund* and ಉಪ್ಪೆ uppe, etc. *Future Tense* of ಉಪ್ಪುನಿ uppuni.)

1st Person.	ಪಂಡ್ದುಪ್ಪೆ paṇḍụduppe, I shall have said.	ಪಂಡ್ದುಪ್ಪಯೆ paṇḍụduppaye, I shall not have said.
	&c. &c.	&c. &c.

IMPERATIVE MOOD.

Singular.

	Positive.	*Negative.*
1st Person.	ಪಣ್ಕೆ paṇuke, let mo say.	ಪಣಂದೆ ಉಪ್ಪುಗೆ paṇande uppuge, let me not say.
2nd „	ಪಣ್ಲ paṇla (ಪಣ್ paṇu), say, or do thou say.	ಪಣಡ paṇaḍa, do thou not say.
3rd „	ಪಣಡ್ paṇaḍu, let him, her, or it say.	ಪಣಂದೆ ಉಪ್ಪಡ್ paṇande uppaḍu, let him, her, or it not say.

Plural.

1st Person.	ಪಣ್ಕ paṇuka, let us say.	ಪಣಂದೆ ಉಪ್ಪುಗ paṇande uppuga, let us not say.
2nd „	ಪಣ್ಲೆ paṇle, say you, or do you say.	ಪಣಡೆ paṇaḍe, do you not say.
3rd „	ಪಣಡ್ paṇaḍu, let them say.	ಪಣಂದೆ ಉಪ್ಪಡ್ paṇande uppaḍu, let them not say.

CONDITIONAL MOOD.

Singular.

1st Person.	ಪಣ್ತ್ವೆ paṇutve, I should say.	ಪಣ್ತ್ವಯೆ paṇutvaye, I should not say.
2nd „	ಪಣ್ತ್ವ paṇutva, thou wouldst say.	ಪಣ್ತ್ವಯ paṇutvaya, thou wouldst not say.
	&c. &c.	&c. &c.

The rest are regular.

94. 6th Conjugation of Verbs ending in ಪಿ pi.

Crude form: ಪರ್ಪಿ **parpi**, to drink.

INDICATIVE MOOD.

PRESENT TENSE.

Singular.

	Positive.	*Negative.*
1st Person.	ಪರ್ಪೆ **parpe**, I drink.	ಪರ್ಪುಜಿ **parpuji**, I do not drink.
2nd "	ಪರ್ಪ **parpa**, thou drinkest. &c. &c.	ಪರ್ಪುಜ **parpuja**, thou doest not drink. &c. &c.

Plural.

1st Person.	ಪರ್ಪ **parpa**, we drink.	ಪರ್ಪುಜ **parpuja**, we do not drink.
2nd "	ಪರ್ಪರ್ **parparu̥**, you drink. &c. &c.	ಪರ್ಪುಜರ್ **parpujaru̥**, you do not drink. &c. &c.

PAST TENSE.

IMPERFECT.

Singular.

1st Person.	ಪರಿಯೆ **pariye**, I drank.	ಪರಿಜಿ **pariji**, I did not drink.
2nd "	ಪರಿಯ **pariya**, thou drankest. &c. &c.	ಪರಿಜ **parija**, thou didst not drink. &c. &c.

Plural.

	Positive.	*Negative.*
1st Person.	ಪರಿಯ pariya, we drank.	ಪರಿಜ parija, we did not drink.
2nd „	ಪರಿಯರ್ pariyarụ, you drank.	ಪರಿಜರ್ parijarụ, you did not drink.
	&c. &c.	&c. &c.

PERFECT.

Singular.

1st Person.	ಪರ್ತೆ partə, I have drunk.	ಪರ್ತಿಜಿ partiji, I have not drunk.
2nd „	ಪರ್ತ parta, thou hast drunk.	ಪರ್ತಿಜ partija, thou hast not drunk.
	&c. &c.	&c. &c.

Plural.

1st Person.	ಪರ್ತ parta, we have drunk.	ಪರ್ತಿಜ partija, we have not drunk.
2nd „	ಪರ್ತರ್ partarụ, you have drunk.	ಪರ್ತಿಜರ್ partijarụ, you have not drunk.
	&c. &c.	&c. &c.

FUTURE TENSE.

1st FUTURE.

Singular.

	Positive.	*Negative.*
1st Person.	ಪರುವೆ **paurve,** I shall drink.	ಪರಯೆ **paraye,** I shall not drink.
2nd „	ಪರುವ **paruva,** thou wilt drink.	ಪರಯ **paraya,** thou wilt not drink.
	&c. &c.	&c. &c.

Plural.

1st Person.	ಪರುವ **paruva,** we shall drink.	ಪರಯ **paraya,** we shall not drink.
2nd „	ಪರುವರ್ **paruvarụ,** you will drink.	ಪರಯರ್ **parayarụ,** you will not drink.
	&c. &c.	&c. &c.

IMPERATIVE MOOD.

Singular.

1st Person.	ಪರ್ಕೆ **parụke,** let me drink.	ಪರಂದೆ ಉಪ್ಪುಗೆ **parande uppuge,** let me not drink.
2nd „	ಪರ್ಲ **parụla** (ಪರ್ **parụ**), drink, or do thou drink.	ಪರಡ **paraḍa,** do thou not drink.
	&c. &c.	&c. &c.

Plural.

1st Person.	ಪರ್ಕ **parụka,** let us drink.	ಪರಂದೆ ಉಪ್ಪುಗ **parande uppuga,** let us not drink.
2nd „	ಪರ್ಲೆ **parụle,** drink you or do you drink.	ಪರಡೆ **paraḍe,** do you not drink.
	&c. &c.	&c. &c.

The remaining regular.

95. **Causative form of Verbs.**

1. Verb ending in ಆವು **āvu.**

Crude form: ಮಳ್ಪಾವು **maḷpāvu,** to cause to make.

INDICATIVE MOOD.

Remark: The Present and Future tenses are the same in the Positive form, but different in the Negative.

PRESENT TENSE.

Singular.

		Positive.	*Negative.*
1st Person.		ಮಳ್ಪಾವೆ **maḷpāve,** I cause to make.	ಮಳ್ಪಾವುಜಿ **maḷpāvuji,** I do not cause to make.
2nd „		ಮಳ್ಪಾವ **maḷpāva,** thou causest to make.	ಮಳ್ಪಾವುಜ **maḷpāvuja,** thou doest not cause to make.
3rd „	*Mas.*	ಮಳ್ಪಾವೆ **maḷpāve,** he causes to make.	ಮಳ್ಪಾವುಜೆ **maḷpāvuje,** he does not cause to make.
„ „	*Fem.*	ಮಳ್ಪಾವಳ್ **maḷpāvaḷu,** she causes to make.	ಮಳ್ಪಾವುಜಳ್ **maḷpāvujaḷu,** she does not cause to make.
„ „	*Neut.*	ಮಳ್ಪಾವುಂಡು **maḷpāvuṇḍu,** it causes to make.	ಮಳ್ಪಾವುಜಿ **maḷpāvuji,** it does not cause to make.

PAST TENSE.

IMPERFECT.

1st Person.	ಮಳ್ಪಾಯೆ **maḷpāye,** I caused to make.	ಮಳ್ಪಾಯಿಜಿ **maḷpāyiji,** I did not cause to make.
2nd „	ಮಳ್ಪಾಯ **maḷpāya,** thou causedst to make.	ಮಳ್ಪಾಯಿಜ **maḷpāyija,** thou didst not cause to make.
	&c. &c.	&c. &c.

PERFECT.

Singular.

	Positive.	*Negative.*
1st Person.	ಮಳ್ಪಾದೆ **maḷpāde,** I have caused to make.	ಮಳ್ಪಾದಿಜಿ **maḷpādiji,** I have not caused to make.
2nd „	ಮಳ್ಪಾದ **maḷpāda,** thou hast caused to make.	ಮಳ್ಪಾದ್ಜ **maḷpāduja,** thou hast not caused to make.
	&c. &c.	&c. &c.

FUTURE TENSE.

1st Person.	ಮಳ್ಪಾವೆ **maḷpāve,** I shall cause to make.	ಮಳ್ಪಾವಯೆ **maḷpāvaye,** I shall not cause to make.
2nd „	ಮಳ್ಪಾವ **maḷpāva,** thou wilt cause to make.	ಮಳ್ಪಾವಯ **maḷpāvaya,** thou wilt not cause to make.
	&c. &c.	&c. &c.

IMPERATIVE MOOD.

1st Person.	ಮಳ್ಪಾವುಗೆ **maḷpāvuge,** let me cause to make.	ಮಳ್ಪಾವಂದೆ ಉಪ್ಪುಗೆ **maḷpāvande uppuge,** let me not cause to make.
2nd „	ಮಳ್ಪಾಲ **maḷpāla,** do thou cause to make.	ಮಳ್ಪಾವಡ **maḷpāvaḍa** (ಮಳ್ಪಾವಂದೆ ಉಪ್ಪುಲ **maḷpāvande uppula**), do thou not cause to make.
	&c. &c.	&c. &c.

INFINITIVE MOOD.

PRESENT TENSE.

1st Infinitive.

ಮಳ್ಪಾವುನಿ **maḷpāvuni,** (to) cause to make.	ಮಳ್ಪಾವಂದೆ ಉಪ್ಪುನಿ **maḷpāvande uppuṇi,** not (to) cause to make.

PAST TENSE.

IMPERFECT AND PERFECT.

Positive.	*Negative.*
ಮಳ್ಪಾಯಿನಿ malpāyini (ಮಳ್ಪಾಯಿನೇ malpāyinē), (to) have caused to make. ಮಳ್ಪಾದಿನಿ malpādini (ಮಳ್ಪಾದಿನೇ malpādinē), (to) have had caused to make.	ಮಳ್ಪಾವಂದೆ ಇತ್ತಿನಿ malpāvande ittini, not (to) have caused to make.

2nd Infinitive (Supine).

ಮಳ್ಪಾವೆರೆ malpāvere, to cause to make.	ಮಳ್ಪಾವಂದೆ ಉಪ್ಪೆರೆ malpāvande uppere, not to cause to make.

2. Verbs ending in ಡು ḍu, are inflected like ಬೂರುನಿ būruni.

Auxiliary Verbs.

96. There are only two Auxiliary Verbs in Tuḷu; viz: ಆಪಿನಿ āpini, to become, and ಉಪ್ಪುನಿ uppuni (or ಇಪ್ಪುನಿ ippuni), to be; ಆಪಿನಿ apini is inflected like ತೂಪಿನಿ tūpini.

Conjugation of ಉಪ್ಪುನಿ uppuni, to be.

97. Of this Verb there exist in the Present tense two forms; the second one seems to have been taken from the Canarese Defective Participial form ಉಳ್ಳ uḷḷa, being.

INDICATIVE MOOD.

PRESENT TENSE.

Singular.

	Positive. 1st Form.	2nd Form.	*Negative.* 1st Form.	2nd Form.
1st Person.	ಉಪ್ಪುವೆ uppuve,	ಉಳ್ಳೆ uḷḷe, I am.	ಉಪ್ಪುಜಿ uppuji,	ಇಜ್ಜಿ ijji, I am not.
2nd "	ಉಪ್ಪುವ uppuva,	ಉಳ್ಳ uḷḷa, thou art.	ಉಪ್ಪುಜ uppuja,	ಇಜ್ಜ ijja, thou art not.
3rd " *Masc.*	ಉಪ್ಪುವೆ uppuve,	ಉಳ್ಳೆ uḷḷe, he is.	ಉಪ್ಪುಜೆ uppuje,	ಇಜ್ಜೆ ijje, he is not.
" " *Fem.*	ಉಪ್ಪುವಳ್ uppuvaḷụ,	ಉಳ್ಳಳ್ uḷḷaḷụ, she is.	ಉಪ್ಪುಜಳ್ uppujaḷụ,	ಇಜ್ಜಳ್ ijjaḷụ, she is not.
" " *Neut.*	ಉಪ್ಪುಂಡು uppuṇḍu,	ಉಂಡು uṇḍu, it is.	ಉಪ್ಪುಜಿ uppuji	ಇಜ್ಜಿ ijji, it is not.

Plural.

	Positive 1st Form	2nd Form	Negative 1st Form	2nd Form
1st Person.	ಉಪ್ಪುವ uppuva,	ಉಳ್ಳ uḷḷa, we are.	ಉಪ್ಪುಜ uppuja,	ಇಜ್ಜ ijja, we are not.
2nd "	ಉಪ್ಪುವರ್ uppuvarụ,	ಉಳ್ಳರ್ uḷḷarụ, you are.	ಉಪ್ಪುಜರ್ uppujarụ,	ಇಜ್ಜರ್ ijjarụ, you are not.
3rd " *Masc.*	ಉಪ್ಪುವೆರ್ uppuverụ,	ಉಳ್ಳೆರ್ uḷḷerụ	ಉಪ್ಪುಜೆರ್ uppujerụ,	ಇಜ್ಜೆರ್ ijjerụ
" " *Fem.*	ಉಪ್ಪುವೆರ್ uppuverụ,	ಉಳ್ಳೆರ್ uḷḷerụ } they are.	ಉಪ್ಪುಜೆರ್ uppujerụ,	ಇಜ್ಜೆರ್ ijjerụ } they are not.
" " *Neut.*	ಉಪ್ಪುವ uppuva,	ಉಳ್ಳ uḷḷa	ಉಪ್ಪುಜ uppuja,	ಇಜ್ಜ ijja

PAST TENSE.

IMPERFECT.

Singular.

	Positive.	*Negative*
1st Person.	ಇತ್ತೆ itte, I was.	ಇತ್ತಿಜಿ ittiji, I was not.
2nd „	ಇತ್ತ itta, thou wast.	ಇತ್ತಿಜ ittija, thou wast not.
3rd „ *Masc.*	ಇತ್ತೆ itte, he was.	ಇತ್ತಿಜೆ ittije, he was not.
„ „ *Fem.*	ಇತ್ತಳ್ ittaḷu, she was.	ಇತ್ತಿಜಳ್ ittijaḷu, she was not.
„ „ *Neut.*	ಇತ್ತ್ಂಡ್ ittuṇḍu, it was.	ಇತ್ತಿಜಿ ittiji, it was not.

Plural.

1st Person.	ಇತ್ತ itta, we were.	ಇತ್ತಿಜ ittija, we were not.
2nd „	ಇತ್ತರ್ ittaru, you were.	ಇತ್ತಿಜರ್ ittijaru, you were not.
3rd „	ಇತ್ತೆರ್ itteru, they were.	ಇತ್ತಿಜೆರ್ ittijeru, they were not.

Remark: ಇತ್ತೆ itte, is the past tense form of ಇಪ್ಪುನಿ ippuni, which is used in some parts of the Tuḷu country besides ಉಪ್ಪುನಿ uppuni.

PERFECT TENSE.

Singular.

1st Person.	ಇತ್ತ್‌ದೆ ittụde, I have been.	ಇತ್ತ್‌ದಿಜಿ ittụdiji, I have not been.
	&c. &c.	&c. &c.

Plural.

	Positive.	Negative.
1st Person.	ಇತ್ತ್ದ ittụda, we have been.	ಇತ್ತ್ದಿಜ ittụdija, we have not been.
	&c. &c.	&c. &c.

FUTURE TENSE.

Singular.

1st Person.		ಉಪ್ಪೆ uppe, I shall be.	ಉಪ್ಪಯೆ uppaye, I shall not be.
2nd „		ಉಪ್ಪ uppa, thou wilt be.	ಉಪ್ಪಯ uppaya, thou wilt not be.
3rd „	*Masc.*	ಉಪ್ಪೆ uppe, he will be.	ಉಪ್ಪಯೆ uppaye, he will not be.
„ „	*Fem.*	ಉಪ್ಪೆಳ್ uppaḷụ, she will be.	ಉಪ್ಪಯಳ್ uppayaḷụ, she will not be.
„ „	*Neut.*	ಉಪ್ಪು uppu, it will be.	ಉಪ್ಪಂದ್ uppandụ, it will not be.

Plural.

1st Person.		ಉಪ್ಪ uppa, we shall be.	ಉಪ್ಪಯ uppaya, we shall not be.
2nd „		ಉಪ್ಪರ್ upparụ, you will be.	ಉಪ್ಪಯರ್ uppayarụ, you will not be.
3rd „	*Masc.*	ಉಪ್ಪೆರ್ upperụ } they will be.	ಉಪ್ಪಯೆರ್ uppayerụ } they will not be.
„ „	*Fem.*	ಉಪ್ಪೆರ್ upperụ } they will be.	ಉಪ್ಪಯೆರ್ uppayerụ } they will not be.
„ „	*Neut.*	ಉಪ್ಪ uppa } they will be.	ಉಪ್ಪಯ uppaya } they will not be.

IMPERATIVE MOOD.

Singular.

	Positive.	*Negative.*
1st Person.	ಉಪ್ಪುಗೆ **uppuge,** let me be.	ಉಪ್ಪಂದೆ ಉಪ್ಪುಗೆ **uppande uppuge,** let me not be; I will not be.
2nd „	ಉಪ್ಪುಲ **uppula,** be thou, or do thou be.	ಉಪ್ಪಡ **uppaḍa,** be not, or do thou not be.
3rd „	ಉಪ್ಪಡ್ **uppaḍụ,** let him, her or it be.	ಉಪ್ಪಂದೆ ಉಪ್ಪಡ್ **uppande uppaḍụ,** let him, her or it not be.

Plural.

1st Person.	ಉಪ್ಪುಗ **uppuga,** let us be.	ಉಪ್ಪಂದೆ ಉಪ್ಪುಗ **uppande uppuga,** let us not be.
2nd „	ಉಪ್ಪುಲೆ **uppule,** be you, or do you be.	ಉಪ್ಪಡೆ **uppaḍe,** be not, or do you not be.
3rd „	ಉಪ್ಪಡ್ **uppaḍụ,** let them be.	ಉಪ್ಪಂದೆ ಉಪ್ಪಡ್ **uppande uppaḍụ,** let them not be.

INFINITIVE MOOD.

PRESENT TENSE.

1*st Infinitive.*

ಉಪ್ಪುನಿ **uppuni** (ಉಪ್ಪುನೇ **uppunē**), (to) be.	ಉಪ್ಪಂದೆ ಉಪ್ಪುನಿ **uppande uppuni,** not (to) be.

PAST TENSE.

Positive.	*Negative.*
ಇತ್ತಿನಿ ittini (ಇತ್ತಿನೇ ittinē), (to) have been.	ಉಪ್ಪಂದೆ ಇತ್ತಿನಿ uppande ittini, not (to) have been.
ಇತ್ತ್ದಿನಿ ittuḍini (ಇತ್ತ್ದಿನೇ ittuḍinē), (to) have had been.	

2nd *Infinitive* (*Supine*).

ಉಪ್ಪೆರೆ uppere, to be.	ಉಪ್ಪಂದೆ ಉಪ್ಪೆರೆ uppande uppere, not to be.

GERUNDS AND PARTICIPLES.

PRESENT AND FUTURE.

Ger. ಇತ್ತೊಣ್ಡು ittoṇḍu, being.	ಇತ್ತೊಣಂದೆ ittoṇande, not being.
Part. ಉಪ್ಪು uppu, being, or that is.	ಉಪ್ಪಂದಿ uppandi, not being, that is not.

PAST TENSE.

IMPERFECT.

Part. ಇತ್ತಿ itti, been, or that was.	ಉಪ್ಪಂದಿ uppandi (ಇಜ್ಜ್ಯಂದಿ ijjyandi), not been, that was not.

PERFECT.

Ger. ಇತ್ತ್ದ್ ittuḍu, having been.	ಉಪ್ಪಂದೆ uppande (ಇಜ್ಜ್ಯಂದೆ ijjyande), having not been.
Part. ಇತ್ತಿ itti (ಇತ್ತ್ದಿ ittuḍi), having been, or that has been.	ಉಪ್ಪಂದಿ uppandi, having not been, or that has not been.
&c.	&c.

97. There are few Defective Verbs and a number of such Verbs as are commonly used only in the third person neuter; as:

a., ಕೊಂಡು **koṇḍu** (*Gerund* of the Verb ಕೊಣುನಿ **koṇuni**, to hold), is used in composition only; as: ಕೊಂಡು ಬರ್ಪಿನಿ **koṇḍu barpini**, to bring, ಕೊಂಡು ಪೋಪಿನಿ **koṇḍu pōpini**, to take away (or to bring to another place).

b., ಕರಿಯುನಿ **kariyuni**, to pass by, to be possible, of which only the following forms are used:—

Singular.

Positive.	*Negative.*
Present tense. ಕರಿಯುಂಡು **kariyuṇḍu**, it is possible.	ಕರಿಯುಜಿ **kariyuji**, it is not possible.
Past „ ಕರಿಂಡ್ **kariṇḍu**, it was possible.	ಕರಿಯಿಜಿ **kariyiji**, it was not possible.
Future „ ಕರಿಯು **kariyu**, it will be possible.	ಕರಿಯಂಡ್ **kariyandu**, it will not be possible.
	Part. ಕರಿಯಂದಿ **kariyandi**, that is impossible.

ತರಿಯುನಿ **tariyuni**, to tarry, to stay, of which only the *Gerund* and *Imperative* exist.

Singular.	*Plural.*
Ger. ತರಿದ್ **taridu**, having tarried.	
Imperative. ತರ್ಲ **tarla**, (ತರಿ **tari**), do thou tarry.	ತರ್ಲೆ **tarle** (ತರಿ **tari**), do you tarry.

	Positive.	*Negative.*
Crude Form:	ಉರಿಯುನಿ **uriyuni**, to burn.	
Present tense.	ಉರಿಯುಂಡು **uriyuṇḍu**, it burns.	ಉರಿಯುಜಿ **uriyuji**, it does not burn.
Past „	ಉರಿಂಡ್ **uriṇḍụ**, it burnt.	ಉರಿಜಿ **uriji**, it did not burn.
Future „	ಉರಿಯು **uriyu**, it will burn.	ಉರಿಯಂಡ್ **uriyandụ**, it will not burn.
Crude Form:	ಮುಗಿಯುನಿ **mugiyuni**, to end.	
Present tense.	ಮುಗಿಯುಂಡು **mugiyuṇḍu**, it ends.	ಮುಗಿಯುಜಿ **mugiyuji**, it does not end.
Past „	ಮುಗಿಂಡ್ **mugiṇḍụ**, it ended.	ಮುಗಿಜಿ **mugiji**, it did not end.
Future „	ಮುಗಿಯು **mugiyu**, it will end.	ಮುಗಿಯಂಡ್ **mugiyandụ**, it will not end.

Remark: There is scarcely one Irregular Verb in Tuḷu; but some verbs have two forms in the Imperfect, a regular and an irregular; as:

IMPERFECT.

	Regular.	*Irregular.*
ಬರ್ಪಿನಿ **barpini**, to come,	ಬತ್ತೆ **batte**,	ಬೈದೆ **beide**, or ಬೌದೆ **boude**, came.
ಜೆಪ್ಪುನಿ **jeppuni**, to lie,	ಜೆತ್ತೆ **jette**,	ಜೈದೆ **jeide**, or ಜೌದೆ **joude**, lay.
ಲೆಪ್ಪುನಿ **leppuni**, to call,	ಲೆತ್ತೆ **lette**,	ಲೈದೆ **leide**, called.

FIFTH SECTION: INDECLINABLES.

1. POSTPOSITIONS.

98. 1. Governing one case, viz:—

a., Genitive case of nouns and pronouns:—ಒಟ್ಟುಗು oṭṭugu, with, along with; ಕೈತಳ್ keitaḷụ, near, at hand; ಲೆಕ್ಕ lekka, ಲೆಕ್ಕನೆ lekkane, like, as; ವಿಷಯ viśaya, ವಿಷಯೊಡು viśayoḍu, about, concerning; ಉಳಯಿ uḷayi, inside; ಪ್ರಕಾರ* prakāra, like, as; ಮುಖಾಂತ್ರ mukhāntra, through; ಪಗತೆಗ್ pagategụ, instead of.

b., The Communicative case:—ಒಪ್ಪ oppa, agreeing with, together; as: ಆಯಡೊಪ್ಪ āyaḍoppa (ಆಯಡ āyaḍa+ಒಪ್ಪ oppa), with him.

Remark: "ಒಪ್ಪ" is never used separately, but always in connection with the Communicative case.

2. Governing two cases, viz:—

The Genitive and Dative cases; ಯೆದ್ರ್ yedụrụ, in front of; ಸುತ್ತ sutta, round; ಸುತ್ತುಮುತ್ತ suttumutta, roundabout.

3. Governing three cases, viz:—

The Genitive, Dative and Ablative cases; ದುಂಬು dumbu, in front, before, formerly; ಬೊಕ್ಕ bokka, afterwards; ಹೊರ್ತಂಡೆ hortande, ಹೊರ್ತು hortu, except, besides, without (&c. may follow any case); ತಿರ್ತ್ tirtụ, below; ಮಿತ್ತ್ mittụ, above; ಪಿರವು piravu, behind.

2. CONJUNCTIONS.

99. ಅತ್ತ್ಡ attụḍa, or, but, besides.

ಅತ್ತಂಡೆ attande, besides.

ಹೊರ್ತಂಡೆ hortande, besides.

ಅಂಡ್ಂಡ anduṇḍa, namely, that is, viz.

ಅಂಡಾಂಡ andāṇḍa, if it be so.

---

* As ಪ್ರಕಾರ prakāra is a noun, it is often used without the case; as: ಈ ಪ್ರಕಾರ ī prakāra, this way; ಆ ಪ್ರಕಾರ ā prakāra, that way; ಈ ಪ್ರಕಾರ ಮಳ್ಪುಲ ī prakāra maḷpula, do in this way.

ಅಂಚಾಯಿನೆಡ್ಡಾವರ **anĉāyineḍḍāvara,** therefore, because.

ಆ **ā,** that.

ಆಂಡ **aṇḍa,** but, if, supposing it be so.

ಆಂಡಲಾ **āṇḍalā,** but, at least, though.

ಆವಡ್ **āvaḍụ,** either, or.

ಲೆಕ್ಕ **lekka,** like.

ಇಜ್ಜಿಡ **ijjiḍa,** or, but, besides.

ಇಜ್ಜ್ಯಂದೆ **ijjyande,** without.

ಬೊಕ್ಕ **bokka,** and, after, afterwards.

ನನಲಾ **nanalā,** more, yet, still.

ಯೆಂಚಾಂಡಲಾ **yenĉāṇḍalā,** however, notwithstanding.

ಲಾ **lā,** and, also, even.

ಲಾ ಇಜ್ಜಿ **lā ijji,** ಲಾ ಅತ್ತ್ **lā attụ,** neither, nor.

ಐಕಾದ್ **eikādụ,** therefore.

ಬೋಡಾದ್ **bōḍādụ,** for the sake of.

ಸಹ **saha,** also.

3. INTERJECTIONS.

100. ಅಯ್ಯೊ **ayyo**, ಉರೋ **urō**, ಉಲಪ್ಪ **ulappa**, ಅಯ್ಯಪ್ಪ **ayyappa**, ಓಪ್ಪ **ōppa**, ವಾಪ್ಪ **vāppa** — Expressions of sorrow and pain.

ಅಃ **ah**, ಆಹಾ **āhā**, ಓ **ō**, ಓಹೋ **ōhō**, ಹೇಹೇ **hēhē**, ಅಪ್ಪ **appa** (ದಾನಪ್ಪ **ḍānappa**) — Expressions of surprise, pleasure, admiration, jest or reproach.

ಅಂದಾ andā
ಇಂದಾ indā } O! oh!
ಹೇ hē
ಇಸ್ is
ಚೀಚೀ čīčī
ಛೀ čhī
ಛೀಛೀ čhīčhī

101. 4. PARTICLES.

ಎ e (ಈಯೆ īye) an emphatic particle denoting affirmation.

ಡ ḍa, if (see Remark 3 on page 57).

ಆ ā, ನಾ nā, ಏ ē, denote question or interrogation; as: ಮಳ್ತರಾ? maḷtarā, did you make? ಮಳ್ತನಾ? maḷtanā, didst thou make? ಉಂದು ನೀತಿಯಾ? undu nītiyā, is this righteousness? ಉಂದು ತೋಟನಾ? undu tōṭanā, is this a garden? ಬರೊಡೇ, shall I come?

ದಾನ್ನಾ dānnā (ದಾನೆ dāne+ನಾ nā), denotes doubt, and is commonly placed after the word with the interrogative particle; as: ಉಂದು ಯೆಡ್ಡೆನಾ ದಾನ್ನಾ ಯಾನ್ ಪಿನಯೆ undu yeḍḍenā dānnā yānu pinaye, I do not know whether it is right or not.

ಆ ā, and, also, even.

III. PART: SYNTAX.

1. Chapter: On the Structure of Sentences.

SUBJECT AND PREDICATE.

102. A sentence is a complete thought expressed in words.

103. Every sentence consists of a Subject and a Predicate; as: ಅರಸು ಆಳುವೆ, the king rules; ಕಡಲ್ ಮಲ್ಲೆ ಆದುಂಡು, the sea is large.

104. The Predicate asserts what the Subject does; as: ಅರಸು ಆಳುವೆ, the king rules;—or what it is; as: ರಾಮೆ ಅರಸು ಆದುಳ್ಳೆ,

Rāma is king;—or how it is; as: ಕಡಲ್ ಮಲ್ಲೆ ಆದುಂಡು, the sea is large.

105. The verb must agree with its subject in gender, number and person; as:

Singular.	1st Person	”	ಯಾನ್ ಮಳ್ತೆ, I made.
	2nd	”	ಈ ತೂಯು, thou sawest.
	3rd	”	ಪೊಣ್ಣು ಗೊಬ್ಬುವಳ್, the girl plays.
	”	”	ಕೈ ಮುಗುರುಂಡು, the hand turns.
Plural.	1st Person		ಯೆಂಕುಳು (ನಮ) ಮಳ್ತ, we made.
	2nd	”	ನಿಕುಳು ಪಾತೆರುವರ್, you speak.
	3rd	”	ಜೋಕುಳು ಮಳ್ಪುವೆರ್, the boys do.
	”	”	ಪೆತ್ತೊಳು ಮೇಪ, the cows feed.

106. Exceptions to this rule are the following:—

1. The honorific pronoun of the third person is frequently construed with the predicate in the second person; as: ತನ್‌ಕುಳು ಮಲ್ಲಾರ್, ಯೆನನ್ ದಯೊಟು ನಡಪುಡುಲೆ, you are a great man, treat me kindly.

2. When the subject expresses a number of inanimate things, the verb is regularly put in the singular number even though the subject has the plural form; as: ರಾಶಿ ಇಲ್ಲುಳು ಪೊತ್ತುದು ಪೋಂಡು, a great many houses were burnt.

3. When a sentence contains several nominatives which are followed by one verb only, the rule is as follows:—

a., When there are several nominatives in the singular number, the verb must be put in the plural form; as: ಅಮ್ಮೆಲಾ ಮಗೆಲಾ ಬತ್ತೆರ್, father and son came.

b., When there are several nominatives of different genders the verb must agree with the last one; as: ಆನೆಲಾ ಅರಸುಲಾ ರಾಣಿಲಾ ಬತ್ತೆರ್, the elephant, the king, and the queen came.

c., If the subject consists of two or more personal pronouns, the first person has the precedence of the second and third, and the second has the precedence of the third, whereas the verb is put in the plural; as: ಈಲಾ ಆಯೆಲಾ ಬತ್ತರ್, thou and he came; ಯಾನ್‌ಲಾ ಈಲಾ ಬತ್ತ, I and thou came.

107. When the nominative is a personal pronoun, it is often omitted, the person being implied by the form of the verb; as: ಪೋಪೆ, (I) go; ಮಳ್ಪುಲಾ, do it (thou).

108. In the same way, in certain sentences the verb is omitted; as: ನರಮಾನ್ಯೆಗ್ ಆತ್ಮ (ಉಂಡು), man has a soul; ಪಕ್ಕಿಳೆಗ್ ರೆಂಕೆಳು (ಉಂಡು), birds have wings; ದುಷ್ಟೆರೆಗ್ ಶಿಕ್ಷೆ (ಆಪುಂಡು), the wicked men will receive punishment.

USES OF THE INFLECTED VERBAL FORMS.

A. Present Tense.

109. 1. The present tense chiefly denotes an action, passing at the time in which it is mentioned; as: ಯಾನ್ ಓದುವೆ, I read; ಯಾನ್ ಬದುಕುವೆ, I live.

2. It is used to express determination with regard to a future action; as: ಎಲ್ಲೆ ಬಪೆ, I (shall surely) come tomorrow; ಆಯೆ ಬತ್ತ್ಂಡ ಯಾನ್ ಪೋಪೆ, if he come(s) I (shall) go.

3. In vivid narration it is frequently used instead of the past tense; as: ಆ ಸಮಯೊಡು ಕೊಡಗುದಾಕುಳು ಮಂಗಳೂರುಗು ಬಪೆರ್, ಆಪಗ ಯಾನ್ ಅವುಳು ಉಳ್ಳೆ, at that time the Coorgs came to Mangalore, then I was there.

B. Past Tense.

110. 1. The Imperfect describes past events generally; as: ಉಣಸ್ ಮಳ್ತ, we took our meal; ದೇವಾಲಯೊಗು ಪೋಯೆ, he went to church.—Sometimes it expresses certainty with

regard to an action that is to take place immediately; as: ಆಕುಳು ಬತ್ತೆರ್, they (have come=) do come immediately.

2. The Perfect represents an action as entirely completed; as: ಇಲ್ಲ್‌ನ್ ಬುಡ್ತೆ (ಬುಡುತೆ), I have left the house;—or as prior to a former action; as: ಯಾನ್ ಇಲ್ಲ್‌ಗ್ ಮುಟ್ಟುನಗ ಆಯೆ ಪೋತೆ, when I came to the house, he was gone.

3. The Pluperfect expresses priority to a former action already completed; as: ಸೂರ್ಯೆ ಮೂಡುನಗ ಯಾನ್ ಲಕ್ಕ್‌ದಿತ್ತೆ, when the sun rose, I had risen.

C. Future Tense.

111. 1. The simple future denotes what is to happen in future; as: ನಮ ಮಾತೆರ್ಲಾ ಸೈವ, we shall all die; ಬರ್ಸ ಬರುವು, it will rain.—Sometimes it expresses probability; as: ಆಕುಳು ಕೋಣೆಡ್ ಉಪ್ಪೆರ್, they are likely in the room; ಆಯೆ ಬರುವೆ, he will probably come.

2. The future perfect sometimes expresses priority of an action with regard to a future action, sometimes doubt with regard to a past action; as: ಆಯೆ ಬನ್ನಂಗೆ ಯಾನ್ ಮಳ್ತ್‌ದುಪ್ಪೆ, when he comes, I shall have done it; ಯಾನ್ ತೆಲ್ತ್‌ದುಪ್ಪೆ, it may be I have laughed.

3. The negative form of the future tense is often used to express resolution or emphasis; as: ಯಾನ್ ಮಳ್ಪಯೆ, I shall never do it; ಆಯೆ ಪಣಯೆ, he will never say it; ಬರ್ಸ ಬರಂದ್, it will not rain.

THE IMPERATIVE MOOD.

112. 1. The first person of the Imperative mood is used to express intent with regard to an action; as: ಯಾನ್ ತೂಕೆ, let me see (I will see); ನಮ ಪ್ರಾರ್ಥನೆ ಮಳ್ಪುಗ, let us pray.

2. The second person is used to order, or give commandments; as: ಈ ಪೋಲ, go thou; ನಿಕುಳು ಬಲ್ಲೆ, come you.

3. The third person (ಮಳ್ಪಡ್, ತೂವಡ್, ಬರಡ್, etc.) is rather an optative, though it is also used imperatively; as: ಅಕುಳು ಆ ಬೇಲೆ ಮಳ್ಪಡ್, they shall or may do that work; ಅಕುಳು ಎಡ್ಡೆ ಉಪ್ಪಡ್, may they be (or do) well.

4. The form ಮಳ್ಪೊಡು, ತೂವೊಡು, etc. signifies urgency or necessity of an action; as: ನಿಕುಳು ಬರೊಡು, you must come; ಒಂಜಿ ಇನಾಮು ದಯ ಮಳ್ಪೊಡು, do give us a present.

USES OF THE AUXILIARY VERBS.

113. ಆಪಿನಿ, *to become*, *to be*. The third person singular (neuter) of the future tense (ಆವು, it will become or be) is very generally used in answer to a command, or to the expression of a wish; as: ಪೇಂಟೆಗ್ ಪೋದು ಅರಿ ಕೊಂಡು ಬಲ್ಲ, go to the bazar and bring some rice; ಆವು (it will take place=), very well! The third person of the Imperative is used to express assent; as: ಅಂಚೆನೆ ಆವಡ್, be it so, or may it become so. (Its use as a Conjunction will be treated hereafter.)

114. ಉಪ್ಪುನಿ, *to be*. Added to the present gerund, it expresses continuancy of, or habit with regard to, an action; as: ಓದೊಣ್ದು ಉಪ್ಪುವೆ (or ಉಳ್ಳೆ), I am reading, or I am in the habit of reading. Added to the past gerund, it denotes completion of an action; as: ಮಳ್ತ್ದ್ ಉಳ್ಳೆ, I have done. Added to the infinitive, it signifies intention or readiness with regard to an action; as: ಪೋವೆರೆ ಉಳ್ಳೆ, I am about to go.

115. ಬಲ್ಲಿ (the negative of the affix ಒಲಿ in ಮಳ್ಪೊಲಿ, etc.) denotes inability; as: ಯಾನ್ ಪೋವೆರೆ ಬಲ್ಲಿ, I cannot go. ಆಯಗ್ ಮಳ್ಪೆರೆ ಬಲ್ಲಿ, he cannot do (it).

SUPPLEMENTAL VERBS.

116. To express a continued action, a final verb is added to the gerund of the reflexive verb; as: ಮೀನ್ ನೀರ್‍ಡ್ ಬದ್‍ಕೊಣ್ದು ಉಪ್ಪುಂಡು, the fish is living in the water; ಯಾನ್ ಓದೊಣ್ದು ಪೋಪೆ, I go reading; ಆಯೆ ರಾಗ ಮಳ್ತೊಣ್ದು ಬರ್ಪೆ, he comes singing.

117. Frequently the past gerund with a final verb is used to represent an action in its successive steps of completion; as: ಅಂಗಿನ್ ದೆತ್ತ್‌ದ್ ಪಾಡ್‍ಲ, take off the coat, and put it away; ಆಯೆ ತತ್ತ್‌ದ್ (or ತತ್ತ್) ಪೋಯೆ, he lost the way and went on, or he went astray; ಆಕುಳು ಪರ್‍ದ್ ಬತ್ತೆರ್, they came drunk; ಆಯೆ ಸೈತ್ ಪೋಯೆ, he died.

THE VERBAL FORMS. (VOICES.)

118. In the active form the subject appears as itself acting; as: ಅರಸು ಆಳುವೆ, the king rules.

119. The causative form represents the subject as causing another to act; as: ಅಮ್ಮೆ ತನ ಮಗನ್ ಚಾಕ್ರಿದಾಯಡ ಲೆಪ್ಪಾಯೆ (or ಲೆಪ್ಪುಡಿಯೆ), the father had his son called by his servant.

120. The reflexive form (or middle voice) is generally used when the subject is doing something for its own advantage; as: ಯಾನ್ ಒಂಜಿ ಆಸ್ತಿನ್ ದುಡಿಯೊಂಡೆ, I acquired property for myself.

---

2. Chapter: Of the Complemental Parts of Speech.

121. When the verb by itself does not suffice to convey the entire meaning of some action, it requires to be completed in one or more of the following ways:—

1. By an object; as: ಅರಸು ರಾಜ್ಯೊನು ಆಳುವೆ, the king rules the empire; ವಿಲ್ಲಿಯಾಮ್ ಫ್ರೆಂಚ್‍ದಾಕುಳೆನ್ ಸೋಪಾಯೆ, William defeated the French.

2. By words that express circumstances of time, place, manner, cause, etc.; as:

a., Time—ಆಯೆ ಕೋಡೆ ಬತ್ತೆ, he came yesterday; ಆಯೆ ಬಹಳ ಸಮಯೊಡ್ದಿಂಚಿ ಅಸ್ವಸ್ಥ ಆದುಳ್ಳೆ, he is ill since a long time; ದಿನೊಕು ಮೂಜಿ ಸರ್ತಿ ಉಣ್ಪೆ, he eats thrice a day.

b., Place—ಯಾನ್ ಮಂಗಳೂರುಡು ವಾಸ ಮಳ್ಪುವೆ, I live at Mangalore; ಕಪ್ಪಲ್ ಬೊಂಬಾಯಿಗ್ ಪೋಪುಂಡು, the ship sails for Bombay; ಆಳ್ ಮಡಿಕೇರಿಡ್ದ್ ಬತ್ತಳ್, she came from Mercara.

c., Manner—ಕುದ್ರೆ ಬೀಸ ಪಾರುಂಡು, the horse runs swiftly.

d., Instrument or cause—ಆಯನ್ ಕೈದ್‌ಡ್ದ್ ಕೆರಿಯೆರ್, they killed him with a sword; ಯಾನ್ ಬಡವುಡ್ದು ಸೈಪೆ, I die of hunger; ಕಣ್ಣ್ ತೂಪಿನೆಕ್ಕಾದ್ ಉಂಡು ಮಳ್ತ್ಂಡ್, the eye has been made for seeing; ಆಯೆ ಕೋಪೊಡ್ದು ಮಳ್ತೆ, he acted from anger; ಈ ಗೋಡೆ ಮಣ್ಣ್‌ಡ್ದ್ ಮಳ್ತ್ಂಡ್, the wall is made of mud.

USES OF THE COMPLEMENTAL CASES.

Nominative Case.

122. 1. The nominative case commonly represents the subject and precedes the verb; as: ದೇವೆರ್ ಪಾತೆರಿಯೆ, God spoke; ದಂಡ್ ಜೈಸ್ಂಡ್, the army was victorious.

2. It is also used to express the *factative* object; as: ಆಯನ್ ಅರಸು ಮಳ್ತೆರ್, they made him king; ದೇವೆರ್ ಪಾಪಿಷ್ಟೆರೆನ್ ನೀತಿವಂತೆರ್ ಮಳ್ಪುವೆ, God makes sinners righteous people; ರಾಣಿ ಆಳೆನ್ ಮಗಳ್ ಅಂದ್‌ದ್ ಶೇರಾವೊಂಡಳ್, the queen adopted her as her daughter.

Dative Case.

123. The dative case is used: 1. To express the object to which the action is directed; as: ಬಡವೆರೆಗ್ ಕೊರ್ಲೆ, give to the poor; ತತ್ತ್ರಿನಾಯಗ್ ಬುದ್ಧಿ ಪಣ್ಲ, admonish the evil-doer; ದೇವೆರೆಗ್ ಪೋಡಿಲ, fear God.

2. To denote possession or authority; as: ನರಮಾನ್ಯಗ್ ಆತ್ಮ ಉಂಡು, man has a soul; ಅರಸುಗು ಅಧಿಕಾರ ಉಂಡು, the king has power; ದೇವೆರೆಗ್ ಸರ್ವಶ್ರಾಣ ಉಂಡು, God is almighty.

3. To denote intention or purpose; as: ಆಯೆ ಭಿಕ್ಷೆಗ್ ಕುಳ್ಳಿಯೆ, he was sitting for alms; ಆಳ್ ಪೇರ್‍ಗ್ ಪೋಯಳ್, she went for milk.

4. With words that signify pleasure or displeasure; as: ರಾಗ ಆಯಗ್ ಸಂತೋಷ, singing is pleasant to him; ಮರಣ ಅನೇಕೆರೆಗ್ ದುಃಖ, death is a grief to many.

5. To express price or worth; as: ಯೂದೆ ಯೇಸುನು ಮುಪ್ಪ ರುಪಾಯಿಗ್ ಮಾರಿಯೆ, Judas sold Jesus for thirty rupees; ಆ ಬಂಗಲೆನ್ ಸಾರ ರುಪಾಯಿಗ್ ಮಾರೊಲಿ, that bungalow may be sold for thousand rupees.

6. To denote measure; as: ದಿನೊಕು ಮೂಜಿ ಸರ್ತಿ ಬರ್ಪೆ, he comes thrice a day.

7. To signify time; as: ಬಯ್ಯಗ್ ಬರ್ಪ, we shall come this evening; ರಡ್ಡ್ ಘಂಟೆಗ್ ಪಿದಾಡುವೆರ್, they will start at 2 o'clock.

8. To express motion to a place; as: ಆಯೆ ಮೈಸೂರುಗು ಪೋಯೆ, he went to Mysore; ತುದೆಕುಳು ಕಡಲ್‍ಗ್ ಪೋಪುಂಡು, the rivers flow towards the sea.

9. To show difference, likeness, or distance; as: ಆನೆಗ್‍ಲಾ ಎಲಿಕ್‍ಲಾ ಬಹಳ ಹೆಚ್ಚ್ ಕಡಮೆ, there is a great difference between an elephant and a mouse; ಬೆಂಗಳೂರು ಮದ್ರಾಸ್‍ಗ್-ದೂರ, Bangalore is far from Madras.

10. To signify relationship; as: ಆಯೆ ಯೆಂಕ್ ಮೆಗ್ಯೆ ಬೂರುವೆ, he is my younger brother.

ACCUSATIVE CASE.

124. The accusative case is used with transitive verbs to express the direct object; as: ಯಾನ್ ಆಯನ್ ತೂಪೆ, I see him; ಕಾಯಿನು ಹೇಬೆಲ್‍ನ್ ಕೆರಿಯೆ, Cain killed Abel.

2. Many verbs govern two accusatives; as: ಐಗುಳು ಜೋಕುಳೆನ್ ದೇವೆರೆ ವಾಕ್ಯೊನು ಓದಿಯೆರೆ ಮಳ್ಪುವೆ, the schoolmaster makes the children read the Bible.

Remark: The crude form of the noun is often used instead of the accusative case; as: ದೇವೆರ್ ಜೀವ ಕೊರ್ಪೆ, God gives life; ಕರ್ತಾವಾ, ಯೆಂಕುಳೆಗ್ ದಯ ತೋಜಾಲ, Lord, show mercy on us.

Locative Case.

125. The locative case signifies: 1. situation; as: ಇಲ್ಲ್‌ಡ್ ಉಂಡು, it is in the house.

2. It expresses time; as: ಆ ದಿನೊಟು ಆಯೆ ಸೈತ್ ಪೋಯೆ, he died on that day.

3. It denotes cause; as: ಆಳ್ ಆ ರೋಗೊಡು ತೀರ್‌ದ್ ಪೋಯಳ್, she died of that illness.

4. It is used to express the superlative degree of adjectives; as: ಆನೆ ಮಾತ ಮೃಗೊಳೆಡ್ ಮಲ್ಲವು, the elephant is the largest of all the beasts.

Ablative Case.

126. The ablative case is used:

1. To express the cause or instrument of an action; as: ಬಾಯಿಡ್ದ್ ಪಾತೆರುವ, we speak with the mouth; ಬುದ್ಧಿಡ್ದ್ ಗ್ರಹಿಸೊಣುವ, we understand with the mind.

2. To express the passive voice; as: ಆಯೆಡ್ದ್ ಪೆಟ್ಟ್ ತಿಂದೆ, I was beaten by him; ಆಕುಳು ಇಂಬ್ಯಡ್ದ್ ಮೋಸ ಪಡೆವೊಂಡೆರ್, they were deceived by that fellow.

3. To denote the material of which a thing is composed; as: ನರಮಾನಿ ಧೂಳುಡ್ದು ಉಂಡಾಯೆ, man was made of dust.

4. To express motion from; as: ಕಾಯಿ ಮರೊಡ್ದು ಬೂರುಂಡು, the fruit falls from the tree.

5. To express beginning or origin; as: ಆದಿಡ್ದ್ ಇಂಚಿ, from the beginning, ಪಾಪೊಡ್ದು ಮರಣ ಬತ್ತ್‌ಂಡ್, death has come through sin.

6. To show comparison; as: ಕುದ್ರೆ ಕತ್ತೆಡ್ದ್ ಮಲ್ಲೆ, the horse is bigger than the ass.

Communicative Case.

127. The communicative case is used:

1. With verbs like ಪಣ್ಪುನಿ; as: ಆಯಡ ಪಂಡೆ, I told him.

ಪಾತೆರುನಿ; as: ಆಕುಳೆಡ ಪಾತೆರುವೆ, I speak to them.

ಕೇಣ್ಪುನಿ; as: ನಿಕುಳೆಡ ಕೇಣುವೆ, I ask you.

ನಟ್ಟೊಣುನಿ; as: ದೇವೆರೆಡ ನಟ್ಟೊಣ್ಲ, beseech God.

ವಿಚಾರಿಸುನಿ; as: ಮೋಕುಳೆಡ ವಿಚಾರಿಸುಲ, inquire of them.

2. To show relation; as: ಎಂಕ್ ಆಯಡ ಎಡ್ಡೆ ಉಂಡು, I am on good terms with him; ಆಯಡ ಎಂಕ್ ದಾಲಾ ಇಜ್ಜಿ, I have nothing against him.

Vocative Case.

128. The vocative usually commences sentences; as: ದೇವೆರೇ, ಎಂಕ್ ಸಹಾಯ ಮಳ್ಪುಲ, O God, help me! ಅಮ್ಮಾ, ಬಲ್ಲ, O father, come!

USES OF THE POSTPOSITIONS.

129. Postpositions are used to express more definitely the relation implied by the simple cases.

The relations expressed by them are chiefly the following.

1. Concern (ವಿಷಯು, ಮಿತ್ತ್); as: ಸಮುದ್ರದ ಗುಂಡಿದ ವಿಷಯೊಡು ನಂಕ್ ವಿಶೇಷ ಗೊಂತಿಜ್ಜಿ, concerning the bottom of the sea we do not know much; ಈ ಪಾತೆರದ ಮಿತ್ತ್ ಆಲೋಚನೆ ಮಳ್ಪುವೆ, I will think about this matter.

2. Locality (ಮಿತ್ತ್, ಕೈತಳ್, ಈಪೆದಿಕ್ಕ್, ಆಪೆದಿಕ್ಕ್); as: ಗುಡ್ಡೆದ ಮಿತ್ತ್ ಒಂಜಿ ದೇವಸ್ಥಾನ ಉಂಡು, on the mountain there is a temple;

ಆಯ ಕೈತಳ್ ಆ ಪುಸ್ತಕ ಉಪ್ಪು, that book (will be) must be with him.

3. Direction (ಅಡೆಗ್, ಕೈತಡೆಗ್, ಮುಟ್ಟ, ಪಿರವುಡ್ದು); as: ತುದೆತಾಡೆಗ್ ಪೋಯೆ, he went to the riverside; ನಿಕುಳೆ ಕೈತಡೆಗ್ ಬತ್ತೆ, I came to you; ಊರು ಮುಟ್ಟ ಪಾರಿಯೆ, he ran as far as the village; ಎನ ಪಿರವುಡ್ದು ಬಲ್ಲೆ, come after me, follow me.

4. Time (ಬೊಕ್ಕ, ಮಿತ್ತ್, ದುಂಬು); as: ಮಧ್ಯಾನಡ್ದ್ ಬೊಕ್ಕ ಬರ್ಪೆ, I shall come in the afternoon; ನಡೀರ್ದ ಮಿತ್ತ್ ಪಿದಾಡಿಯೆರ್, they set out after midnight; ಮರಣೊಡ್ದು ದುಂಬು ಮನಸ್ಸ್ ತಿಂಗಾರ್ಲ, repent before death.

5. Measure (ಮುಟ್ಟ); as: ಎಳ್ಪ ಸರ್ತಿ ಏಳ್ ಮುಟ್ಟ ಕ್ಷಮಿಪೊಡು, you must forgive up to seventy times seven.

6. Intention, purpose (ಬೋಡಾದ್); as: ದೇವೆರೆ ರಾಜ್ಯೊಗು ಬೋಡಾದ್ ಪೇಚಾಡ್ಲ, labour for the kingdom of God; ಈ ಸಂಗತಿಗ್ ಬೋಡಾದ್ ಯಾನ್ ಬತ್ತೆ, I came on account of this matter.

7. Agreement (ಪ್ರಕಾರ, ಲೆಕ್ಕನೆ); as: ನೀತಿದ ಪ್ರಕಾರ ನ್ಯಾಯ ತೀರ್ಪುವೆ, he will judge with righteousness; ಆ ಮಾದ್ರಿದ ಲೆಕ್ಕನೆ ಮಳ್ಪುಲೆ, make it according to that pattern.

8. Communion (ಒಪ್ಪ with — construed and always contracted with the communicative case —, ಹೊರ್ತಂದೆ, without, ಒಟ್ಟುಗು); as: ಆಯಡೊಪ್ಪ (or ಆಯು ಒಟ್ಟುಗು) ಪೋಯೆ, I went with him; ಎನ ಹೊರ್ತಂದೆ ನಿಕುಳೆಗ್ ದಾಲಾ ಮಳ್ಪೆರೆ ಬಲ್ಲಿ, without me you cannot do any thing; ಆಯು ಒಟ್ಟುಗು ಕುಳ್ಳೆರೆ ಆವಂದ್, you should not sit with him (or near him).

9. Instrument (ಮುಖಾಂತರ, ಮುಖೊಟು); as: ದೇವೆರ್ ಲೋಕೊನು ತನ ವಾಕ್ಯದ ಮುಖಾಂತ್ರ ಉಂಡು ಮಳ್ತೆ, God created the world by His word.

10. Interchange (ಪಗತೆಗ್, ಬದಲ್‌ಗ್, instead); as: ಅಮ್ಮ ಪಗತೆಗ್ ಮಗೆ ಬತ್ತೆ; the son came instead of his father; ಪ್ರೀತಿಗ್ ಬದಲಾದ್ ಪಗೆ ತೋಜಾಯೆ, instead of love, he showed enmity.

USES OF THE ADVERBS.

130. Adverbs are used to denote the place, time manner or cause of actions.

1. Adverbs denoting place (ಓಳು, ಔಳು, ಇಂಚಿ, etc.); as: ಬೊಂಬಾಯಿ ಓಳು ಉಂಡು, where is Bombay? ಬೊಂಬಾಯಿ ಇಂಚಿ, ಮದ್ರಾಸ್ ಅಂಚಿ, Bombay is here (in this direction), Madras is there (in that direction); ಬರ್ಸದ ಕಾಲೊಡು ತಿರ್ತ್ಡ್ದ್ ಮ್ಯೆಂದ್ ಏರುಂಡು, ಮಿತ್ತ್ಡ್ದ್ ಪನಿಲಾ ಬರ್ಸಲಾ ಬೂರುಂಡು, in the rainy season mist is rising from below, and dew and rain are falling from above.

2. Adverbs signifying time (ಇನಿ today, ಎಲ್ಲೆ tomorrow, ಇತ್ತೆ now, this moment, ಬೊಕ್ಕ afterwards, etc.); as: ಇನಿ ಇತ್ತಿನಾಯೆ ಎಲ್ಲೆ ಪೋವೆ, he who was (here) today will start tomorrow; ಇತ್ತೆ ಬರ್ಸ ಬೊಕ್ಕ ದೊಂಬು, now there is rain, afterwards there will be heat.

Remark: 1. To show the commencement of an action or condition, frequently the adverb is construed with the instrumental case; as: (ಕೋಡೆಡ್ದ್ ಇಂಚಿ or) ಕೋಡೆದ್ದಿಂಚಿ ತರೆ ಬೇನೆ ಉಂಡು, since yesterday I have headache.

2. To express the point of time at which any thing ends or is finished, the adverb takes the form of the dative case; as: ಇನಿಗ್ ಆ ಬೇಲೆ ತೀರುಂಡು, today that work will be done;—or it is coustrued with the postposition ಮುಟ್ಟ; as: ಕಡೆ ಮುಟ್ಟ, to the last; ಇಡೆ ಮುಟ್ಟ, until here (till now); ಅಡೆ ಮುಟ್ಟ, until there; ಇದ ಮುಟ್ಟ ಬತ್ತ್ಜಿ, he did not come till now; ಅಡೆ ಮುಟ್ಟ ಕಾಪೊಡಾ, shall I wait so long? ದೇವೆರ್ ನಮನ್ ಕಡೆ ಮುಟ್ಟ ಕಾಪೆ, God will keep us to the end.

3. Adverbs of mode or manner (ಬೇಗ quickly, ಮೆಲ್ಲ slowly, ಸರ್ತ straightly, ಓರೆ crookedly, etc.); as: ಬೇಗ ಬಲ್ಲ, come quickly; ಮೆಲ್ಲ ನಡಪುಲ, walk slowly; ಸಂತೋಷಾದ್ ಕೊರಿಯೆ, he gave it gladly; ಪೊರ್ಲುದ್ ಆದ್ ರಾಗ ಮಳ್ತೆರ್, they sang nicely.

USES OF THE INFINITIVE, PARTICIPLE AND GERUND.

131. The first infinitive (ಮಳ್ಪುನಿ to make, ತೂಪಿನಿ to see etc.) is frequently used for the inflected verbal forms; as: ಏರ್ ಬತ್ತಿನಿ, who has come? ಯೆಂಕುಳು ಬತ್ತಿನಿ, we have come.

132. The second infinitive (supine) is used as the object to a transitive verb; as: ಆಕುಳೆನ್ ಬುಡುಪಾವೆರೆ ಆಯ ಅಪೇಕ್ಷೆ, his desire is to deliver them; ಆಳ್ ಪರಿಯೆರೆ ಕೇಂಡಳ್, she asked for drink (lit. drinking).

Remark: The gerund is frequently added to the supine without altering the meaning; as: ಕೊಂಡಾಯೆರೆ ಆದ್ ಬತ್ತ, we came to receive something; also the dative affix ಗ is sometimes added to it; as: ಮಳ್ಪೆರೆ ಪೋಯಿ, I went to do it.

133. The participle has frequently the meaning of an adjective or a relative sentence; as: ಆಯೆ ಮಳ್ಪ ಬೇಲೆ, his work, the work he is doing; ನಮ ತೂಯಿ ಮರ, the tree we have seen.

134. The gerund is used 1. to express actions in their succession; as: ಎಸಾವು ತಿಂದ್‍ದ್, ಲಕ್ಕದ್, ಪಿದಾಡ್ದ್ ಪೋಯೆ, Esau ate, rose and went away.

2. To denote the mode how an action is performed; as: ಆಯೆ ತೆಲಿತೊಂಡ್ದ್ ಬತ್ತೆ, he came laughing; ಆಕುಳು ತೆರಿದ್ ಸುಳ್ಳು ಪಂಡೆರ್, they willingly told a lie.

3. To express the reason or cause of actions; as: ಆಣ್ ಕಲ್ಪಂದೆ ಶೆಟ್ಟಿಯೆ, this boy was ruined by not learning; ಘಾಳಿ ಬತ್ತ್‍ದ್ ಪಂದ್‍ಗ ಬೂರ್‍ಂಡ್, the fruits fell down through the blowing of the wind.

4. To express time; as: ಈ ಊರುಗು ಬತ್ತ್‍ದ್ ಆಜಿ ವರ್ಷ ಆಂಡ್, it is six years since I came to this place.

135. Participial and verbal nouns are treated like other nouns; as: ನೆರ್ಪಿನವು ಪಾಪ ಆದುಂಡು, abusing is a sin; ನೆರ್ಪಿನೆತ್ತ ಫಲ ನಾಚಿಗೆ ಆದುಪ್ಪುನಿ, the fruit of abusing is shame; ಸೈಪಿನೆಕ್ ಪೋಡಿಗೆ ಉಂಡು, they are afraid of dying; ಆಕುಳು ಮಳ್ತಿನೆಕ್ ದಾನೆ ಪಣ್ಪಿನಿ, what may be said about their doings?

3. Chapter: Of the Attributive Parts of Speech.

136. Pronominal attributes.

1. Interrogative; as: ವಾ ನರಮಾನಿ, which man? ಎಂಚಿತ್ತಿ ಕುದುರೆ, what kind of horse?

2. Demonstrative; as: ಈ ಸಾದಿ, this way; ಇಂಚಿತ್ತಿ ಕೊಡೆ, such an umbrella; ಆ ಪೆತ್ತ, that cow; ಅಂಚಿತ್ತಿ ಇಲ್ಲ್, such a house.

137. Numeral attributes; as: ಆಜಿ ಮಂದೆ, six persons; ಮೂಜನೆ ಸಂಧಿ, the third chapter; ಪಾಕ ರುಪಾಯಿ, some rupees; ಬೊಕ್ಕೊಂಜಿ ಕೋರಿ, another fowl.

138. Qualitative attributes; as: ಎಡ್ಡೆ ಕುಂಟು, a nice cloth; ಸಣ್ಣ ಮರ, a small tree; ಶುದ್ಧ ನೀರ್, clean water.

139. Participial attributes; as: ಪಿಲಿನ್ ಕೆರಿ ಜವನ್ಯೆ, the young man who killed the tiger; ಜವನ್ಯೆ ಕೆರಿ ಪಿಲಿ, the tiger which was killed by the young man; ಅರಸು ಆಯಿ ದಾವೀದ್, the king David (or David who had become king); ಅಮ್ಮೆ ಆಯಿ ದೇವೆರ್, God the father; ಬುದ್ಧಿ ಇಜ್ಜಂದಿ ಆಣ್, the boy who had no understanding; ಬುದ್ಧಿ ಇತ್ತಿ ಆಣ್, an intelligent boy; ಯಾಕೋಬ್ ಇನ್ಪಿ ನರಮಾನಿ, the man named Jacob; ಸಿಂಹ ಇನ್ಪಿ ಮೃಗ, the animal called lion.

140. The particle ಆತ್, is often affixed to nouns and partiples, and the compound is then used attributively; as: ಜನತಾತ್ ಬುದ್ಧಿ, as many men so many minds; ಕಲ್ಲ್‌ದಾತ್ ಭಂಗಾರ್, so much gold as stone; ಬತ್ತಿನಾತ್ ಮಂದೆ, so many men as have come; ಆಯೆ ಪೋಯಿನಾತ್ ದೂರ, the distance he went.

---

4. Chapter: Construction.

ORDER OF WORDS.

141. 1. The subject always precedes the predicate; as: ಅರಸು ಆಳುವೆ, the king rules; ಲೋಕ ಮಲ್ಲವು, the world is large.

2. Words which form the completion of the verb as objects, adverbs, etc. precede the verb; as: ಅರಸು ರಾಜ್ಯೊನು ಆಳುವೆ, the king rules the kingdom; ಅರಸು ರಾಜ್ಯೊನು ಬುದ್ಧಿಡ್ದ್ ಆಳುವೆ, the king rules the kingdom with wisdom; ದುಷ್ಟೆರ್ ದೇವೆರೆನ್ ವಾ ಕಾರಣೊಡ್ದು ನಂಬುಜೆರ್, for what reason do the wicked not believe in God? ಒಂಜಿ ದಿನೊಟು ಒಂಜಿ ಆಣ್ ಸಾಲೆಡ್ ಪರೀಕ್ಷೆಗ್ ಲೇಖನಿಡ್ದ್ ಒಂಜಿ ಕಾಗಜಿನ್ ಬರೆಯೆ, one day a boy wrote a letter with a quill for examination at school.

3. In the same way, attributes, or words necessary to complete the subject or object, must precede these; as: ಎಡ್ಡೆ ನರಮಾನಿ, a good man; ಬಹಳ ಮಲ್ಲ ಕುದುರೆ, a very big horse; ಆಣ ಅಮ್ಮ ತೋಟದ ಗುವೆಲ್ದ ನೀರ್ ಎಡ್ಡೆ ಉಂಡು, the water of the boy's father's well is good; ಯಾನ್ ಒಂಜಿ ಪೊರ್ಲು ಕಥೆನ್ ಓದಿಯೆ, I read a nice story.

CONNECTION OF CO-ORDINATE WORDS.

142. When several co-ordinate words are used in a sentence in the same case, the affix by which the case is formed is only added to the last one, and this has the plural form; as: ಜಿಲ್ಲೆ, ಊರು, ಗ್ರಾಮೊಳೆಡ್ ಅಧಿಕಾರಿಳು ಉಳ್ಳೆರ್, there are officers in districts, towns and villages.

143. Sometimes different co-ordinate words are joined together by a demonstrative pronoun; as: ನೋವೆ, ಆಯ ಬೊಡೆದಿ, ಆಯ ಮೂವೆರ್ ಮಗಾಡ್ಳು, ಮೋಕುಳೆ ಬೊಡೆದಿಯಾಡ್ಳು, ಈ ಎಣ್ಮ ಮಂದೆ ಜಲಪ್ರಳಯೊಡು ಒರಿಯೆರ್, Noah, his wife, his three sons, and their wives, these eight persons were spared in the deluge.

Remark: Repetition of words is employed:—

1. To represent a collective notion in its constituent parts; as: ಆಯಾಯ ಕ್ರಿಯೊಳೆ ಪ್ರಕಾರ ಕೊರ್ಪೆ, he gives to every one according to his deeds; ಒರಿ ಒರಿ ತನ ತನ ವಿಷಯೊಡು ಜವಾಬುದಾರೆ, every one is responsible for himself; ಭಿಕ್ಷೆಗಾರೆ ದೇಶ ದೇಶೊಗು ಸಂಚರಿಸ್ದ್ ಊರು ಊರುಡು ತಿಂಗೊರ್ಳ್ಗು, ಇಲ್ಲ್ ಇಲ್ಲ್‌ಗ್ ಪೋಪೆ, the

beggar is travelling from country to country, roving from village to village, going from house to house.

2. To denote intensity; as: ಮಲ್ಲ ಮಲ್ಲ ಕಪ್ಪಲುಲು ದೂರ ದೂರ ಸೀಮೆಗ್ ಪೋಪುಂಡು, very large vessels are sailing to a very far country; ಪಂಡ್‌ಪಂಡ್ ಸಾಕಾಂಡ್, I told him until I became tired.

USES OF CONJUNCTIONS.

144. Copulative conjunctions (ಲಾ, ಬೊಕ್ಕ, ಆಂಡಲಾ, ಆವಡ್); as: ಯಾನ್ ಪೋಪೆ ಈಲಾ ಬರೊಡು, I am going, come you too; ಪ್ರೀತಿಲಾ ದಯಲಾ ದೇವೆರೆ ಸ್ವಭಾವ, love and grace are God's nature; ಆಯಗ್ ಪೇರ್ ಬೊಕ್ಕ ಸಕ್ಕರೆ ಪಾಡ್ದ್ ಕೊರಿಯ, we gave him milk and sugar; ಮಿತ್ತ್ ಆಕಾಶೊಡು ಆಂಡಲಾ, ತಿರ್ತ್ ಭೂಮಿಡ್ ಆಂಡಲಾ, ಭೂಮಿದ ತಿರ್ತ್ ನೀರ್‌ಡ್ ಆಂಡಲಾ, ಉಪ್ಪುನೆತ ವಿಗ್ರಹ ಮಳ್ತ್‌ದ್ ಐಕ್ ಸಾಷ್ಟಾಂಗ ಬೂರಿಯೆರೆ ಆವಂದ್, of any thing that is in heaven above or that is in the earth beneath or that is in the water under the earth thou shalt not make an idol nor bow before it; ಕಾಂಡೆ ಆವಡ್ ಬೈಯ್ಯ ಆವಡ್ ಬರ್ಪೆ, I shall come in the morning or in the evening.

145. Disjunctive conjunctions (ಅತ್ತ್, ಅತ್ತಂದೆ, ಹೊರ್ತು, ಹೊರ್ತಂದೆ, ಅತ್ತ್‌ಡ, ಅತ್ತಾಂಡ and ಇಜ್ಜಿಡ, ಇಜ್ಜಾಂಡ); as: ಕೆಂಪುದವು ಅತ್ತ್‌ಡ ಬೊಳ್ದುದವು ಕೊಂಡು ಬಲ್ಲ, bring me a red one or a white one; ಗಂಜಿ ಇಜ್ಜಿಡ ನುಪ್ಪು, gruel or rice; ಪ್ರಧಾನಿ ಅತ್ತ್, ಅರಸು ಯಜಮಾನೆ, not the minister but the king is master; ಪಾಪಿಷ್ಠೆರೆಗ್ ಶಿಕ್ಷೆ ಅತ್ತಂದೆ ನಾಚಿಗೆಲಾ ಆಪುಂಡು, sinners will get shame besides punishment; ದೇವೆರೆ ವಾಕ್ಯ ಹೊರ್ತು ಬೇತೆ ಸತ್ಯ ಶಾಸ್ತ್ರ ನಂಕ್ ಇಜ್ಜಿ, besides the word of God we have no other sacred scripture.

USES OF SOME PARTICLES.

146. Emphatic particle (ಏ, ಯೇ, ವೇ, ನೇ) "ಏ" is generally used after a final ಉ or ್; as: ಆಯೆ ಪಂಡಿನವು ಸುಳ್ಳೇ, what he told was a lie; ಇಲ್ಲೇ ಮಗ್‌ರ್ಂಡ್, even the house tumbled down.

"ಯೇ" is generally used after a final ಇ or ಎ, sometimes

after ಉ; as: ದೇವೆರೆಗ್ ಮೆಚ್ಚುನವು ಪ್ರೀತಿಯೇ, ಪ್ರಜೆನ್ ಯೇರಾವುನವು ನೀತಿಯೇ, what God delights in is love, it is righteousness that exalts a nation.—"ನೇ" is generally used after a final ಅ, sometimes after ಎ; as: ಆಯೆ ಯೆಂಕ್ ಕೊರಿನವು ಒಂಜಿ ಪುಸ್ತಕನೇ, what he gave me was a book; ಆಯೆನೇ ಬರಡ್, he himself is to come.—"ವೇ" is generally used after a final ಉ; as: ಗುರುವೇ ಬತ್ತಿನಿ, the priest has come.

147. Interrogative particles (ಆ, ಒ, ಯಾ, ನಾ, ವಾ, and ಏ ನೇ, ವೇ). Euphonically these are treated like the emphatic particles, explained in the previous paragraph; as: ಪ್ರೀತಿಯಾ, is it love? ಬರಿಯಾ, is it a wall? ಸುಳ್ಳಾ, is it a lie? &c.

With regard to their signification "ಆ" or "ನಾ" are used in simple questions; as: ಯಾನ್ ಬರೊಡಾ, shall I come? ಮಳ್ತರಾ, have you done it? ತೂಯನಾ, have you seen it?—and "ಏ" or "ನೇ" is used when the answer is expected to be a negation of what has been asked; as: ಯಾನ್ ಬರೊಡೇ, shall I come? ಬರೊಡ್ಚಿ, do not come.

---

5. Chapter: Connexion of Sentences.

CO-ORDINATE SENTENCES.

148. Co-ordinate sentences are sometimes put together without formal connexion; as: ಸೂರ್ಯ ಪ್ರಕಾಶ ಕೊರ್ಪುಂಡು, ಐತ ರವಿಳು ಭೂಮಿದ ಮಿತ್ತ್ ಬೂರುಂಡು; ಐತ ದೊಂಬುಡ್ದು ಪಾದೆ ಕಲ್ಲ್ ಕಾಯುಂಡು, the sun is shining, its beams are falling on the earth, (and) from its heat the rocks are heated.

149. More frequently, however, they are joined together by the use of conjunctions; as: ನರಮಾನಿ ಪುಟ್ಟುನಗ ಕುಳ್ಳಿಯೆರೆ ಬಲ್ಲಿ, ಐಡ್ದ್ ಬೊಕ್ಕ ನಡಪೆರೆ ಕಲ್ಪುವೆ, ನನ ಪಾಕ ಸಮಯದ ಮಿತ್ತ್ ಪಾತೆರಿಯೆರೆ ಸುರು ಮಳ್ಪುವೆ, when man is born he is not able to sit, afterwards he learns to walk, and after some time begins to

speak; ಅನೇಕೆರೆಗ್ ಯೆಡ್ಡೆ ಉಪಾಯ ಗೊಂತುಂಡು, ಆಂಡಲಾ ಅವೆನ್ ನಡಪುಡಿಯೆರೆ ಆಕುಳೆಗ್ ಸಾಮರ್ಥ್ಯ ಇಜ್ಜಿ, many people know (have) good means, but they are not able to employ them; ನರಮಾನ್ಯೆರ್ ಪಾಪೊಡು ಬೂರಿಯೆರ್, ಐಕ್ ಬೋಡಾದ್ ಆತ್ ಕಷ್ಟ ಪಡೆವೊಣುವೆರ್, men have fallen into sin, therefore they are suffering so much; ಆಯಗ್ ಬೇಸರ ಉಂಡು, ದಾಯೆಗಂದ್ಂಡ ಆಯೆ ದೂರ ನಡತೆ, he is tired, for he has come from a great distance.

SUBORDINATE SENTENCES.

150. Incomplete subordinate sentences (which are formed by the use of the uninflected verbal forms) are either adjectival or adverbial.

1. *Adjectival sentences* qualify nouns; as: ಯಾನ್ ತೂಪಿ ಮರ ಎತ್ತರ ಆದುಂಡು, the tree which I see is high; ಈ ಕೆಲಸೊನು ಮಳ್ತಿ ನರಮಾನಿ ಬಹಳ ಬುದ್ಧಿನ್ ತೋಜಾಯೆ, the man that did this work displayed much sense.

2. *Adverbial sentences*, like adverbs, qualify verbs and express time, place, manner or cause; as:

a., Time: ಧರ್ಮರಾಜೆ ಆಳೊಣ್ದು ಉಪ್ಪುನಗ ಪ್ರಜೆಳು ಸುಖೊಟು ಇತ್ತ್ಂಡ್, as long as Dharmarāja was ruling, the people lived happily; ಯಾನ್ ಬರ್ಪಿನೆಕ್ ದುಂಬು ಆಯೆ ಪೋಯೆ, before I came he went away; ಪೆಟ್ಟ್ ತಿಂದಿ ಮಿತ್ತ್ ಬುದ್ಧಿ ಬತ್ತ್ಂಡ್, after he was punished he became wise; ಆಕುಳು ಬರ್ಪಿ ಮುಟ್ಟ ಆಯೆ ಓದೊಣ್ದು ಇತ್ತೆ, he was reading until they came; ಆಯೆ ಬನ್ನಂಗೆ ಆಕುಳು ಕಾತೆರ್, they were waiting until he arrived.

b., Place: ಕಲ್ಲ್ ಬೂರಿನವುಳು ಒಟ್ಟೆ ಆಂಡ್, where the stone struck there a hole was made.

c., Mode: ನಿನ ಚಿತ್ತ ಪರಲೋಕೊಡು ಆಪಿ ಲೆಕ್ಕನೆ ಭೂಮಿದ ಮಿತ್ತ್ ಆವಡ್, thy will be done in earth as it is in heaven.

d., Cause: ನರಮಾನ್ಯೆರ್ ಪಾಪ ಮಳ್ತಿನೆಡ್ದ್ ಕಷ್ಟ ಅಲ್ಂಭವಿಪುವೆರ್, because men have sinned (therefore) they suffer.

151. Complete subordinate sentences are either relative, conditional, or direct.

1. *Relative sentences* are connected with their principal sentence by the use of the relative and demonstrative pronouns and the particle "ಅ" or "ನ್"; as: ಏರ್ ಪಾಪ ಮಳ್ಪುವೆನಾ ಆಯೆ ಐತ ಫಲ ತಿನ್‍ಂಬೆ, he who commits sin will eat the fruit of it; ಅಪ್ಪೆ ಅಮ್ಮೆ ಎಂಚಿತ್ತಿನಾಕುಳಾ ಅಂಚಿತ್ತಿನಾಕುಳು ಬಾಲೆಳು, as parents are, so will be their children; ಪುಣ ಓಳು ಉಂಡಾ ಅವುಳು ಕರುಕುಳು, the eagles will be gathered where the carcass is.

2. *Conditional sentences* are joined to their principal sentences by the affix "ಡ"; as: ಬರ್ಸ ಬತ್ತ್‍ಂಡ ಯಾನ್ ಪೋವಯೆ, if there be rain, I shall not go; ಸಮಾದ್ ಕಲ್ಪುವಡ ನಿಕ್ಕ್ ಒಂಜಿ ಇನಾಮು ತಿಕ್ಕು, if you learn well, you will get a present; ಆಯೆ ಮೂಳು ಇತ್ತ್‍ದ್ವಿಡ ಈ ಆಪತ್ತ್ ಎಂಕ್ ಆತ್ವಂದ್, if he had been here, this misfortune would not have befallen me.

3. *Direct sentences* are either adjectival or substantival.

a., *Adjectival direct sentences* are joined to their principal sentences by the use of the verbal form "ಇನ್ನಿ"; as; ಆಯೆ ಕಂಡೊಂಡೆ ಇನ್ನಿ ಸುದ್ದಿ ಎಂಕ್ ಬಹಳ ದುಃಖ ಕೊರ್ಪುಂಡು, I am much grieved to hear that he has committed theft.

b., *Substantival direct sentences* are joined to their principal sentences by the use of the verbal nouns "ಇನ್ನಿನವು" or, in the case of quotations, by the gerund "ಅಂದ್ದ್"; as: ದೇವೆರ್ ಸರ್ವತ್ರಾಣ ಇತ್ತಿನಾಯೆ ಇನ್ನಿನವು ಮಾತೆರೆಗ್ ತೆರಿಯುಂಡು, ಆಂಡ ಆಯೆ ಪರಿಶುದ್ಧದಾಯೆ ಆದುಳ್ಳೆ ಇನ್ನಿನೆಕ್ಕ್ ಒಪ್ಪಿಯೊಣ್‍ಂಡ ತನುಕುಳೆಗ್ ತನುಕುಳೇ ನ್ಯಾಯ ತೀರ್ಪೊಣ್‍ದ್ವೆರ್ ಇನ್ನಿನವು ಪಿಂಬೆರ್, all know that God is almighy, but they do not admit that He is holy, because they know that, if they did so, they would judge themselves; ದೇವೆರ್ ತೂಪೆ ಅಂದ್ದ್ ಮಾತೆರ್ಲಾ ಪಣ್ಪೆರ್, ಆಂಡ ಅವು ಸತ್ಯ ಅಂದ್ದ್ ನಂಬುನಾಕುಳು ಒಂತೆ ಮಂದಿ, all say that God is seeing, but few only believe it.

APPENDIX.

A. Specimens of the dialect of the Tuḷu Brahmins.

1. Examples of different expressions for the same thing:

a. Common Tulu.	*b. Brahmins' Dialect.*
ಆಣ್ āṇụ,	ಮಾಣಿ māṇi, boy.
ಪೊಣ್ಣು poṇṇu,	*ಜೋವು jōvu, girl.
ಈಯವು īyavu,	ಪಾಪು pāpu, enough.
ಈಯಂದ್ īyandụ,	ಪಾಪನ್ pāpanụ, not enough.
ಬೊಕ್ಕ bokka,	ಬೆತ್ತ್ bettụ, afterwards.
&c.	&c.

2. Words with changed Consonants:

ಉಣ್ಪು uṇpu,	ಉಂಪು umpu, meal.
ದಾನೆ dāne,	ಜಾನೆ jāne, what?
ದಾಲ dāla,	ಜಾಲ jāla, any thing.
ದಾಯೆಗ್ dāyegụ,	ಜೇಯೆಗ್ jēyegụ, why?
ಬೊಡ್ಚಿ boḍči,	ಬೋತ್ರಿ bōtri, not wanted.
ಬತ್ತೆಗೆ battege,	ಬತ್ತೆಕೆರೆ battekere (or ಕೇರ್ kērụ), it is said he came.
ಲೆಪ್ಪುನಿ leppuni,	ವೊಲೆಪ್ಪುನ voleppuna, (to) call.
ದಪ್ಪುನಿ dappuni,	ಅಡಪ್ಪುನ aḍappuna, (to) plough.
ಮಳ್ಪುನಿ maḷpuni,	ಮಂಪುನ mampuna, (to) make.
ಮಳ್ಪುವೆ maḷpuve,	ಮಂಪುವೆ mompuve, I make.
ಮಳ್ತೆ maḷte,	ಮಂತೆ mante, I made.
ಮಳ್ಪೆ maḷpe,	ಮಂಪೆ mampe, I shall make.
ಹೃದಯೊಗು hrụdayogu,	ಹೃದಯೊಂಕು hrụdayoṅku, to the heart.
ಹೃದಯೊಡು hrụdayoḍu,	ಹೃದಯೊಂಟು hrụdayoṇṭu, in the heart.
ಉಣಸ್‌ಗ್ uṇasụgụ,	ಉಣಸ್‌ಂಕ್ uṇasụṅkụ, to dinner.
ಉಣಸ್‌ಡ್ uṇasụḍụ,	ಉಣಸ್‌ಂಟ್ uṇasụṇṭụ, at dinner.

* "ಜೋವು" is also used for child in general by the Holeyas, and the plural "ಜೋಕುಳು, children" is common to all.

B. Tuḷu Poetry

1. According to metrical rules.

(Tuḷu Brahmin's Dialect.)

ಅಂದ ದೇವೆರೇ ಈರೆಗೆನಟೇತ್ ಕೋಪೊ ಜಾಯೆಕ್ ಯೆಂದಳ್
ಇಂದಿರಾಧವ ನಿತ್ಯ ಸ್ನೇಹಿತೆ ಯೆಂದ್‌ಸ್ತುತಿತಳ್ ಆರೆನಿ ।
ಚಂದ್ರಕಲೆಕುಳೆ ಧರಿತಿ ಈರೆ ಮುಖಾಂಬುಜೋಂತ ಯೆದ್‌ರ್‌ಟ್ ।
ಚಂದೊಂಟಿನಣೇರ್ ಚೂತು ಅಂಗೀಕಾರೊ ಮಂತೊಣೊಡಂದಳ್ ॥ ೫೧ ॥

ಮದನಾರಿ ಚೂತು ತನ ಕಾಂತೆಡೊಪ್ಪ ಕುಳ್ಳಿಯೆರ್ ।
ತದನಂತರೊಂಟು ನಂದೀಶ್ವರೆಲ ಬತ್ತ್‌ತ್ ಈಶ್ವರಗ್ ।
ಪದೊಂಕುಳೆಗ್ ಅಭಿವಂದಿತ್ ಪುಡವಾಡ್‌ತ್ ಪ್ರಮಥೆರೆಗ್ ।
ಅಧಿಪತಿಯೆಂದ್ ಪಣ್ಪೊತಿನಾಯೆ ಬತ್ತೆದೆರೆಂತ್‌ನಗ ॥ ೫೨ ॥

ನಾರದ ಮುನಿಂದ್ರ ವಚನೊಂಕುಳೆನಿ ಕೇಂಡ್‌ತ್ ।.
ಸಾರ ಹೃದಯೊಂಟು ರತಿ ದುಃಖೊ ಬುಡುನಗಲಾ ।
ನಾರಾಯಣ ಶ್ರೀಚರಣೊ ಭಕ್ತಿಡ್ ದೃಢಿತೊಂಡು ।
ಸ್ವೈರೊ ಸುಖಿತ್‌ತ್ತೆರ್ ನಾಣನಿತ್ಯೊ ವಿಭವೊಂಟು ॥ ೫೩ ॥

ಪಾಪಿ ತಪೊಚೆಟ್ಟೋತ್ತೆ ಯೆಂದ್ ಮನಸ್‌ಟ್ ಯೆಂಣ್‌ತ್ ।
ಶ್ರೀಪತಿಗ್ ಭಕ್ತಿಡ್ ಸಮರ್ಪಣೊನಿ ಮಂತ್ । ಶಂಭು ।
ಸ್ಥಾಪಿತ್‌ಣ ವೊತ್ತ್ರಳ್‌ತ್ ಚೋಜನ ಪ್ರಕಾರ ।
ರೂಪೊ ಮದೆಮಂತ್ ಶಿವೆಯಾತ್ರಿತೆರ್ ಅಳ್ತ್ ॥ ೫೪ ॥

2. Folksong.

(Common Tuḷu.)

ಆಕನಪಾಡಿನಿಪಿ ಆವದಿಕೆ ಆಯ ಅಪ್ಪೆನಾ ।
ತಾಕೊಟೆದ ಬೆಜಕ್‌ರೆ ಅರವಾರೆ ಒಂಜ ಬರುವೆರ್ ।
ಆ । ಆವಡಾನೆ ಕಟ್ಟೆ ಪಂಬದನವು ।
ಕಾರಗೆಜ್ಜ ಗಗ್ಗರ ಕೇಣುಂಡೇ ನಂಕ್ ।
ಆವ ಮನ್‌ಸೆದಿಗ್ ಕೇಣ್‌ಂಡ್ ।
ಆ । ಐಯ್ಯೊ ಮಗಾ ಕನಪಾಡಿಯೆ ಕೇಂಡನಾ ।
ನಮ ಊರ ಪಾಡಿದಾರ್ ನೇಲುವೆರ್‌ಯೇ ।

ಆ | ಆವಡಾನೆ ಆವಮನ್‌ಸೆದಿ ತುಂಡಿನೆಡ್ದ್ |
ಕನಪಾಡಿದಾಯೆ ಯೆಂದ್ ಪುದರ್ ಆಂಡ್ |
ಆ | ಆವದೈವ ಬರುವೆ ನಟ್ಟ ನಡೀರ್‌ಡ್ |
ಜಾವೊಂದ ಪೊರ್ತುಡು ಬರುವೆನಯೇ |
ಆ | ಒಳವೂರ ಬೂಡುಗುಗೆ ಬರುವೆನೊ |
ಇಂದು ಒಂಜಿ ರಾಜ್ಯೊಡು ಯೆಂಕ್ ಸಾನ ಕಟ್ಟ್ |
ನೇಮಬಲಿಯೆ ಬೋಡುಂದೆ |
ನೆರಡ ಪಣ್‌ಕೆ ಪುಲ್ಲ್ಯನಗ ನಂಕ್ ||

C. Tuḷu Proverbs.

1. ಅಂಡೆದ ಬಾಯಿ ಕಟ್ಟೊಲಿ, ದೊಂಡೆದ ಬಾಯಿ ಕಟ್ಟೊಲ್ಯಾ?

Literal Translation: Of a vessel the mouth may be tied up, of the throat, the mouth can it be tied up?

Meaning: The mouth of a vessel may be tied up, but can a man's tongue be kept quiet?

2. ಅಂದಾಯಿ ಪಾತೆರೊಗು ಸಂದಾಯ ಇಜ್ಜಿ.

Lit. Tr. True being to a word reply is not. *Mean.* A right answer turns away all obstacles..	Truth makes free.

3. ಅಜ್ಜಿ ತಾಂಕಿ ಮಗೆ ಬೊಜ್ಜೊಗುಲಾ ಆವಯೆ.

Lit. Tr. The grandmother brought up son, for the performing obsequies will not be fit.

Mean. A son brought up by the grandmother will become unfit for anything.

4. ಅಳೆಕ್ ಬತ್ತಿನಾಯಗ್ ಎರ್ಮೆದ ಕ್ರಯ ದಾಯೆಗ್?

Lit. Tr. For buttermilk, he that came, of the cow, the price why?
Mean. What business has he who came for buttermilk, to ask the price of the cow?

Engl. prov. Meddle not with that you have nothing to do withal!

5. ಉಪ್ಪು ತಿಂದಿನಾಯೆ ನೀರ್ ಪರ್ವೆ.

Lit. Tr. Salt, he who ate, water will drink.

Mean. He who ate salt will drink water.

Germ. prov. Wer A sagt muss auch B sagen.—Wer den Teufel in's Boot geladen hat, muss ihn auch über's Meer fahren.

6. ಎಣ್ಣಿನವು ಮಂಣ್ ಆಂಡ್, ಪೆದ್ದಿನವು ಪೊಂಣು ಆಂಡ್.

Lit. Tr. What he expected dust it became, what was born a girl it was.

Mean. His expectations were not fulfilled, what was born, is a girl.

Germ. prov. Seine Hoffnung ist in's Wasser gefallen; or: Berge kreisen und gebären Mäuse.

7. ಒಕ್ಕೆಲ್ಮೆ ಮಳ್ತಿನವು ದಂಡೊಗು, ಬ್ರಾಣೆ ಮಳ್ತಿನವು ಪಿಂಡೊಗು; ಮನ್ಸೆ ಮಳ್ತಿನವು ಹೆಂಡೊಗು.

Lit. Tr. The Bant, what he has done, for fine; the Brahmin, what he has done, for ceremonial balls; the Holeya, what he does, for drinking.

Mean. The Bant's earning is spent on law-suits, the Brahmin's earning on ceremonies, the Holeya's on drink.

8. ಕಂಬುರ್ಜ ಶೀಪೆ ಅಂದ್ದ್ ಬೇರ್ ಮುಟ್ಟ ಅಗ್ಗಿಯಡ.

Lit. Tr. Sugarcane sweet, having said, the root until do not eat.

Mean. Because the sugarcane is sweet, you must not eat its root also.

Germ. prov. Man muss des Guten nicht zu viel thun.

9. ಕಟ ಜಾತಿಗ್ ಬಡು ಜಾತಿ.

Lit. Tr. To draught cattle, the beating stick.

Mean. Draught cattle want beating.

10. ಕಾಡ್ ಸೊರ್ಕಿನವುಳು ಏಡ್ನ್ ಬುಡೊಡು, ಊರು ಸೊರ್ಕಿನವುಳು ಕೊಂಕಣನ್ ಬುಡೊಡು.

Lit. Tr. The forest where it is fat the goat you must let go, the village, where it is fat the Konkaṇas you must let go.

Mean. Where the forest is fat you must put the goat, where a village is prospering you must let the Konkaṇas go in.

11. ಕಾಲೊಗು ತಕ್ಕ ಕೋಲ, ದೇಶೊಗು ತಕ್ಕ ಭಾಷೆ, ತಾಳೊಗು ತಕ್ಕ ಮೇಳ.

Lit. Tr. For the time suitable the game, for the country suitable the language, for the drum suitable the dancing.

Mean. According to the time must be the feast (or game) of the demon; according to the country is its language; according to the music must be the dance.

12. ತನ ತರೆಕ್ ತನ ಕೈ.

Lit. Tr. To his forehead his hand.
Mean. He has no help but his own.

Engl. prov. God gives us hands, but does not build bridges for us.

13. ತಾನ್ ಕಳುವೆ ಆಂಡ ಊರು ಕಳುವೆಗೆ.

Lit. Tr. He himself a thief, if (he) is the village a thief be.

Mean. If he himself is a thief, he think the whole village to be full of thieves.

Engl. prov. Every one measures other people's corn by his own bushel.

Germ. prov. Der Dieb meint sie stehlen alle.

14. ತಾನ್ ಮಳ್ತಿನವು ಉತ್ತಮು, ಮಗೆ ಮಳ್ತಿನವು ಮಧ್ಯಮು, ಆಳ್ ಮಳ್ತಿನವು ಹಾಳ್.

Lit. Tr. He himself what he did, the best, the son what he did, middling, the cooly what he did, bad.

Mean. What one does himself is well done, what the son does is not so well done, but what the servant does is done badly.

Engl. prov. If a man will have his business well done, he must do it himself.

Germ. prov. Selbst thuts ganz, heissen zur Hälft, und Bitten gar nicht.

15. ನಲಿಪೆರೆ ತೆರಿಯಂದಿನಾಯಗ್ ಜಾಲ್ ವ್ಪೋರೆಗೆ.

Lit. Tr. To dance, to him that does not know, the floor is uneven they say.

Mean. He who does not know to dance says the floor is uneven.

16. ನಾಯಿದ ಬೀಲ ವ್ಪೋಂಟೆಡ್ ಪಾಡ್ಂಡ ಸಮ ಆವಾ?

Lit. Tr. Of the dog the tail in a tube if you put, straight will it become?

Mean. Will a dog's tail become straight by putting it into a tube?

Engl. prov. A bargain is a bargain.

Germ. prov. Was man nicht kann meiden, soll man williglich leiden.

17. ಪಜೆ ಇತ್ತಿನಾತ್ ಕಾರ್ ನೀಡೊಡು.

Lit. Tr. The mat, as far as it is, the feet one must stretch.

Mean. According to the mat you must stretch your feet.

Germ. prov. Man muss die Füsse nach der Decke strecken.

18. ಪಲ್ಲಡ್ ಕುಳ್ಳುದು ಪರಂಟ್ ಪತ್ತ್ಯೆ.

Lit. Tr. In the pit having sat, young frogs he caught.

Mean. Sitting in the pit, he caught young frogs.

Germ. prov. Sie schlagen die Sehnecken auf die Sehwäntze damit sie nicht shreien.

19. ಪಿಜಿನ್‌ಗ್ ದಾಯೆಗ್ ಕರ್ಬದ ಬೇಲೆ?

Lit. Tr. For the ants why iron work?

Mean. What business has the ant with the blacksmith's work?

20. ಬಾಯಿಡ್ ಮಗ, ಮಗ! ಬಂಜಿಡ್ ಭಗ, ಭಗ!

Lit. Tr. In the mouth, darling, darling! in the belly envy, envy!

Mean. The words are sweet, but the mind is bitter.

21. ಬೆರಿಕ್ ಬೂರಿ ಪೆಟ್ಟ್‌ಲಾ ಕಬೊರ್ಗು ಕೊರಿ ನೀರ್‌ಲಾ ಪಿರ ಬರುವಾ?

Lit. Tr. On the back fallen blows, to the iron put water will it return?

Mean. The blows given on the back, and the water put on hot iron in order to harden it can never be taken back.

Germ. prov. Diese nimmt ihm kein Jude mehr ab.

22. ಬಂಟೆರ್ ಪೋಯಿನವುಳು ನ್ಯಾಯ ತಪ್ಪಂದ್, ಮಡೆಂಜಿ ಪೋಯಿನವುಳು ಕಳಂಕ್ ತಪ್ಪಂದ್.

Lit. Tr. The Bants, where they come, quarrel will not fail, *madenji* fish where it comes silt will not fail.

Mean. Where Bants are there is quarrel, where the *madenji* fish is, there is silt.

23. ಮೆಲ್ಲಾಯಗ್ ಬಾಸೆ ಪಣಿಯೆರೆ ಆವಂದ್, ಬಡವಗ್ ಆಶೆ ತೋಜಾವೆರೆ ಆವಂದ್.

Lit. Tr. The rich man reproach to tell is not allowed, the poor hope to tell is not allowed.

Mean. Do not blame the rich, and make not the poor hope.

Germ. prov. Bei grossen Herren muss man fünf gerad sein lassen.

24. ಮಾದಿಗ ಇಲ್ಲ್‌ಡ್ ಉಣಸ್ ಆಂಡ ಬ್ರಾಣಗ್ ದಾನೆ?

Lit. Tr. Of the cobbler, in the house, a dinner if there is, to the Brahmin what?

Mean. What profit has a Brahmin of a dinner in a cobbler's house?

25. ಮಲ್ಲ ಪುದೆ ಮೆಲ್ಲ ಜಾವೊಡು.

Mean. A heavy load you must put down slowly.

26. ಮಾಮಿ ದರ್ತಿ ಕರಕ್ ಬಿಲೆ ಇಜ್ಜಿ.

The vessel broken by the mother-in-law did cost nothing.

27. ಮಂಗ ಕೈಟ್ ಮಾಣಿಕ ಕೊರಿ ಲೆಕ್ಕ.

It is as if you gave a ruby to a monkey.

28. ಯೆರುತ ಬೇನೆ ಕಕ್ಕೆಗ್ ದಾನೆ ತೆರಿಯುಂಡು?

Does the crow understand, or feel, the pain of the buffalo?

29. ಯೇರಿನ್ ತಿಂದ್ದ್ ಬೋರಿನ್ ಮಾರಿಯೆ.

Having eaten the *yēri* fish, he sold the bullock.

30. ಯೇಳೆಡೊಂಜಿ ಮರ್ಲ್ ಯೇಳ್ಪೆಡೊಂಜಿ ಮರ್ಲ್.

As children of seven years are foolish, so are people of seventy years.

31. ಯೆನನ್ ಈ ಕರ್ಂಟಾನಗ ನಿನನ್ ಯಾನ್ ಕರ್ಂಟಾವೆ.

If you tease me, I shall tease you.

32. ರೊಟ್ಟಿ ಕೊಣೊಯಿ ನಾಯಿ ನೆಯಿ ನಟ್ಟೆಯೆರೆ ಬರುವಾ?

Will the dog which took away bread ask for ghee?

33. ರೊಟ್ಟಿ ದೆಕ್ಕ್‌ದ್ ನೀರ್ ಪರ್ಪಿನಿ.

Having washed the bread, he drinks the water.

34. ರಾತ್ರೆಡ್ ತೂಯಿ ಉಗ್ಗೆಲ್‌ಡ್ ಪಗೆಲ್‌ಡ್ ಬೂರಿ ಲೆಕ್ಕ.

In daylight he fell into the well which he saw at night.

35. ರೋಗಿಗ್ ವೊಂಜೇ ಸಂಕಡ, ಇಲ್ಲ್‌ದಾಕುಳೆಗ್ ಒಂರ್ಭ ಸಂಕಡ.

The sick one has only one sickness, but the inmates of his house have nine.

36. ಲೆಖ್ಖೊಗು ದುಃಖ ಇಜ್ಜಿ ಇನ್ನಿ ಲೆಕ್ಕ.

In clearing up the account there is no grief.

37. ವೊಕ್ಕೆಲುಳೆ ಜುಟ್ಟ್ ಗುತ್ತಿಗೆದಾಯ ಕೈಟ್.

The tuft of the tenant is in the hand of his landlord.

38. ವರಣ್‌ಗ್ ಬಡ್ಡಿ ಇಜ್ಜಿ, ಪೆತ್ತಗ್ ಅಳೆಪಾಯಿ ಇಜ್ಜಿ.

For money no interest, for the cow no rent.

39. ವೋಡೊಗು ಆಪಿ ಮರನ್ ಕೀಲ್‌ಗ್ ಆವಂದಿ ಲೆಕ್ಕ ಮಳ್ತೆ.

A tree fit for a boat he scratched so much that it cannot be used even for a bolt.

40. ಒಂಜಿ ಕೆಬಿಟುಂಡುಡ ಏಕಾಂತ, ರಡ್ಡ್ ಕೆಬಿಕ್ ಬೂರ್ಂಡ ಲೋಕಾಂತ.
What one ear heard is secret, what two ears heard is public.

41. ಶೆಟ್ಟಿ ಬೊಕ್ಕ ಬುದ್ಧಿ, ಸೈತಿ ಬೊಕ್ಕ ದುಃಖ.
After ruin one gets understanding, after death grief.

42. ಶೆಟ್ಟಿ ಬುಡಿನಾಳೆ ಪಟ್ಣ.
Where the headman is, there is the town.

43. ಸತ್ಯನೇ ಗತಿ, ಧರ್ಮನೇ ಜಯ.
Truth is support, virtue is victory.

44. ಸತ್ಯ ನೀರ್ಡ್ ಮುರ್ಕಂದ್ ತೂಟು ಪೊತ್ತಂದ್.
Truth cannot be drowned nor burnt.

45. ಸಾದಿಡ್ ಪೋತಿ ಮಾರಿನ್ ತನ ಮಿತ್ತ್ ಪಾಡೊಂಡೆ.
The plague which was wandering on the road he took upon himself.

46. ಸೈತಿ ಎರ್ಮೆಗ್ ಪೇರ್ ದಿಂಜ.
The dead cow had given much milk.

47. ಸಾರ ಕಕ್ಕೆಗ್ ಒಂಜಿ ಬಿರು.
For a thousand crows one bow (is enough to drive them away).

48. ಹಳ್ಳಿ ದೇವೆರೆಗ್ ಕೊಳ್ಳಿ ದೀಪ.
To the village-god live-coals must represent the lamp.

49. ಹೇಡಿ ಕೈಟ್ ಚಂದ್ರಾಯುಧ ತಿಕ್ಕಿ ಲೆಕ್ಕ.
It is as if you gave the discus to a coward.

50. ಹೆಡ್ಡೆ ಶೆಟ್ಟನವು ಇಜ್ಜಿ, ಜಾಣೆ ಬಾಳಿನವು ಇಜ್ಜಿ.
A fool will not be ruined, a wise man will not prosper.

INDEX.

I. PART: PHONOLOGY.

Page

1. CHAPTER: **Of the Alphabet** . . . 1
   a., Of Vowels . . . 1
   b., Of Medials . . . 1
   c., Of Consonants . . . 1

2. CHAPTER: **Of Pronunciation** . . . 2
   a., Vowels . . . 2
   b., Consonants . . . 3
   c., Syllables . . . 6
   d., Double Consonants . . . 6

3. CHAPTER: **Of Euphony** . . . 7
   a., Elision . . . 7
   b., Insertion . . . 7
   c., Permutation . . . 7

II. PART: ETYMOLOGY.

1. CHAPTER: **Of the Formation of Words** . . . 8
   Distinction of Words according to their Origin . . . 8
   Distinction of Words according to their Form . . . 8
   a., Primitive Words . . . 8
   b., Derivative Words . . . 9
      1. Verbal Derivatives . . . 9
      2. Other Derivatives . . . 9
   c., Compound Words . . . 9

2. CHAPTER: **Of Parts of Speech** . . . 10
   First Section: Nouns . . . 10

Page

1. Of Substantives 10
   a., Gender of Substantives 10
   b., Number of Substantives . . 10
   c., Declension of Substantives . . 11
   Nouns of Relationship 28
   Verbal Nouns . . 30
2. Of Adjectives . . . 31
   Comparison of Adjectives . . 31
3. Of Adverbs 32

Second Section: Pronouns . . . 32

1. Substantive Pronouns 33
   a., Personal and Demonstrative Pronouns . . 33
   b., Reflexive Pronouns 33
   c., Interrogative Pronouns 34
   d., Indefinite Pronouns 34
2. Adjective Pronouns 34
   a., Demonstrative . . 34
   b., Interrogative 34
   c., Indefinite 34
3. Adverbial Pronouns 35
   a., Demonstrative . . 35
   b., Interrogative 35
   c., Indefinite 36
   Declension of Pronouns 37

Third Section: Numerals . . . 41

1. Substantive Numerals . . 41
2. Adjective Numerals 41
   a., Cardinal numbers 41
   b., Ordinal numbers . 43
3. Adverbial Numerals . . . 43

Fourth Section: Verbs . . 43

1. Forms of the Verb 43
2. Tenses of the Verb 44
3. Moods of the Verb 45
4. Conjugation of the Verb 45

Fifth Section: Indeclinables . . . 111

Page
1. Postpositions 111
2. Conjunctions 111
3. Interjections 112
4. Particles 113

III. PART: SYNTAX.

1. CHAPTER: **On the Structure of Sentences** . 113
Subject and Predicate 113
Uses of the Inflected Verbal Forms . . 115
a., Present Tense 115
b., Past Tense 115
c., Future Tense 116
The Imperative Mood . . 116
Uses of the Auxiliary Verbs 117
Supplemental Verbs 118
The Verbal Forms (Voices) 118

2. CHAPTER: **Of the Complental Parts of Speech** . . . 118
Uses of the Complemental Cases 119
Nominative Case 119
Dative Case 119
Accusative Case 120
Locative Case 121
Ablative Case 121
Communicative Case 122
Vocative Case 122
Uses of the Postpositions . . . 122
Uses of the Adverbs 124
Uses of the Infinitive, Participle and Gerund . 124

3. CHAPTER: **Of the Attributive Parts of Speech** . . . 126
Pronominal Attributes 126
Numeral Attributes 126
Qualitative Attributes 126
Participial Attributes 126

4. CHAPTER: **Construction** 126
Order of Words 126
Connexion of Co-ordinate Words . 127
Uses of Conjunctions 128
Uses of some Particles 128

Page

5. CHAPTER: **Connexion of Sentences** . . 129

Co-ordinate Sentences 129

Subordinate Sentences 130

APPENDIX 132

a., Specimens of the Dialect of the Tuḷu Brahmins. 132

b., Tuḷu Poetry 133

c., Tuḷu Proverbs . . . 134

CORRIGENDA.

(The lines are counted from the top to the bottom.)

Page 6, Line 11: Put "Table showing the alphabet with the combinations of vowels and consonants" at the head of the 4th page.

P. 8, L. 14: Put "(ಶೂನ್ಯ)" behind "ಸೊನ್ನೆ".

P. 9, L. 21: "21" to be omitted.

P. 11, L. 21: Put "ಳಿಗೆ" behind "ರಿಗೆ".

P. „ L. 23: „ "ರಿಡ" „ "ಳಿಡ".

P. „ L. 24: „ "ರಿಡ್ಡ" „ "ಳಿಡ್ಡ".

P. „ L. 25: „ "ರಿದ" „ "ಳಿದ".

P. 33, L. 11: „ „ ಅವು avu, "that" instead of "this".

P. 40, L. 1: "that" after remark to be omitted.

P. 81, L. 5: Put "Subjunctive Mood" instead of "Conditional Form".

P. 111, L. 4: Put, "The" before "Genitive case".

P. 113, L. 4-7: Behind these words put "Expressions of disgust".

P. „ L. 20: Read "ಉ" instead of "ಅ".

P. 120, L. 27: Put "1" behind "124".

P. 124, L. 19: Read "ಞನಿಚ" instead of "ಞನಿಗ".

P. 125, L. 7: Add "ಗ" to "ಮುಳ್ಳಿರ".

P. 136, L. 3: Add "s" to "think".

www.ingramcontent.com/pod-product-compliance
Lightning Source LLC
Chambersburg PA
CBHW030349170426
43202CB00010B/1306
* 9 7 8 3 7 4 3 3 9 3 5 1 6 *